"As someone who grew up in hip-hop culture and as someone who pastors a church targeting it, I can say a book like this is long overdue. For years there has been a tension between the two due to a lack of understanding. This has been an additional factor in the drop in church attendance among emerging generations. Efrem and Phil do a thorough job of breaking down the history of hip-hop culture and the dynamics of urban churches. They paint an encouraging and realistic picture of how the church can engage the culture and stay true to its biblical foundation."

Tommy Kyllonen, a.k.a. Urban D., *lead pastor, Crossover Church, and national hip-hop artist*

"The hip-hop culture has penetrated, infiltrated and influenced greatly the young American culture. Hip-hop is no longer an African American phenomenon but now has greatly impacted the White and Latino culture as well. It is extremely important for us as Christians to understand the art of hip-hop and how we can use this medium to reach young Americans with the good news of Jesus Christ. Phil Jackson and Efrem Smith's new book, *The Hip-Hop Church,* is the best resource I've seen in helping us bridge this gap. For anyone working with youth today, *The Hip-Hop Church* is a 'have to' read."

Wayne "Coach" Gordon, *president, Christian Community Development Association, and founding pastor, Lawndale Community Church*

"Phil and Efrem have shaped a refreshing and insightful look into the world of hip-hop through the lens of the gospel. They are able to discuss hip-hop culture in a way that is theologically sound while also 'keeping it real.' This book is a must-read for pastors, teachers, theologians, youth leaders or anyone else serious about ministry to this current generation."

Rev. Tony Lee, *senior minister to young adults, Ebenezer A.M.E. Church*

"This book is a well-written and concise guide by two men who are familiar with the mores and folkways of the hip-hop culture. It is an excellent tool that will enable the church to encounter and engage this culture as agents of transformation. It also challenges the church to reevaluate who it is and what it is to be about. If the church is to be the most powerful instrument in the public square, then it must imitate the carpenter from Galilee. We must go forth, not in judgment but in love as we dialogue with hip-hop culture. The church can make a difference, and it must. The difference will come when we realize agape is a panacea for our existential situation. Therefore, I highly recommend this book and its authors as chief resources to be read and utilized in claiming this territory yet unconquered."

Dr. Mack King Carter, *senior pastor, New Mount Olive Baptist Church, Fort Lauderdale, Florida*

"Finally! A thorough resource that intelligently articulates what is too often misunderstood."

Gerard Henry, *speaker, author and TV host of BET's* Lift Every Voice

The Hip-Hop Church

CONNECTING WITH THE MOVEMENT SHAPING OUR CULTURE

Efrem Smith and Phil Jackson

IVP Books

An imprint of InterVarsity Press
Downers Grove, Illinois

InterVarsity Press
P.O. Box 1400, Downers Grove, IL 60515-1426
World Wide Web: www.ivpress.com
E-mail: mail@ivpress.com

InterVarsity Press® is the book-publishing division of InterVarsity Christian Fellowship/USA®, a student movement active on campus at hundreds of universities, colleges and schools of nursing in the United States of America, and a member movement of the International Fellowship of Evangelical Students. For information about local and regional activities, write Public Relations Dept., InterVarsity Christian Fellowship/USA, 6400 Schroeder Rd., P.O. Box 7895, Madison, WI 53707-7895, or visit the IVCF website at <www.intervarsity.org>.

All Scripture quotations, unless otherwise indicated, are taken from the New American Standard Bible, copyright 1960, 1962, 1963, 1968, 1971, 1972, 1973, 1975, 1977, 1995 by The Lockman Foundation. Used by permission.

Lyrics to "One Love" by Adam Levin used by permission of the author.

Photos in chapter six courtesy of Forbes Designs.

Design: Cindy Kiple
Images: Duane Reider/Getty Images

ISBN-10: 0-8308-3329-3
ISBN-13: 978-0-8308-3329-0

Printed in the United States of America ∞

Library of Congress Cataloging-in-Publication Data

Smith, Efrem (Efrem D.), 1969-
    The hip-hop church: connecting with the movement shaping our
culture / Efrem Smith and Phil Jackson.
        p. cm.
    Includes bibliographical references.
    ISBN 0-8308-3329-3 (pbk.: alk. paper)
    1. African Americans—Religious life. 2. Hip hop—Religious
    aspects
—Christianity. I. Jackson, Phil, 1964-. II. Title.
    BR563.N4S5735 2005
    261—dc22

                                                            2005021331

P   16   15   14   13   12   11   10   9   8   7   6   5   4   3   2   1
Y   18   17   16   15   14   13   12   11   10   09   08   07   06   05

CONTENTS

Foreword by Bakari Kitwana   7

Foreword by Alton B. Pollard III 12

Shout-Outs. 15

Hip-Hop and the Church: Opposition or Opportunity? 17

PART ONE: Why Should the Church Care About Hip-Hop?

  1 Church and Hip-Hop. 31

PART TWO: Understanding the Hip-Hop Culture

  2 What Is Hip-Hop? 61

  3 Blues and Negro Spirituals, the Parents of Hip-Hop 92

  4 Hip-Hop as Postmodern Culture 101

  5 Hip-Hop Theology 115

PART THREE: Bringing Hip-Hop into Your Church

  6 Holy Hip-Hop. 131

  7 The Emcee and the Preacher. 153

  8 The Deejay and the Worship Leader. 176

  9 Bringing Hip-Hop into Your Worship Service 185

10 Practical Ways of Reaching the
   Hip-Hop Community for Christ 200

Conclusion: Church and Hip-Hop—You Don't Stop 217

Appendix: Hip-Hop Resources 222

FOREWORD

Defining Hip-Hop's Spiritual Philosophy

I've always found the expression "Christian hip-hop" to be a bit of an oxymoron. It's a phrase that seems as loaded with contradiction as, say, the emerging term "hip-hop feminist." But this is what happens when tradition meets the new. It's what happens when generations collide. Much of this whole debate around Christian hip-hop is just that, one of personal preference, generational division and change.

I'm reminded here of a comment Jesse Jackson made in the summer of 1995 at one of the many heights of the recurring national debate over prayer in the public schools. As long as math and physics are taught, Jackson said, as long as there are Thursday night parties and Friday morning exams, there will be prayer in schools. And as long as hip-hop is the culture of today's youth, there will always be hip-hop in the church.

Given the growing list of Christian hip-hop acts and even ministries that cater to hip-hop audiences, the question of whether or not hip-hop has a place in the church is not the real issue. The real question is, how can a more meaningful dialogue be nurtured between the two? Answering this question requires give-and-take on both sides.

Those in the church who are resistant to hip-hop there need to confront at least a few of the many misconceptions about hip-hop.

For example, those skeptical of hip-hop should understand that hip-hop is more than just music. Hip-hop music is just one aspect of a youth culture that speaks to a larger lifestyle. Hip-hop skeptics must also realize that true hip-hop is more than just what they hear and see on the radio and television. Too often these media depend on sensational images to secure their market position. They are not trying to preserve the art and culture of hip-hop. Hence they magnify sex and drugs and glorify the anti-authority and materialistic components of hip-hop. In the process, they define, albeit inaccurately, hip-hop for those outside the culture. But hip-hop isn't by nature all decadent. It's a mode of expression that tends to be a bit more gritty and edgy as it attempts to find a voice in a mainstream culture that has too long denied young people their say.

Likewise, young people into hip-hop who feel strongly about its place in the church have got to do their part to make hip-hop work for hardcore churchgoers. Few would dispute that hip-hop can be brought into the church as is. But it may not be enough to simply change the message and keep the packaging. Those who would bridge hip-hop with Christianity must grapple with the contradictions that hip-hop poses for a Christian lifestyle.

The rapper Mase (one of the biggest stars on P. Diddy's rap label, Bad Boy), who left the hip-hop world at the height of his success in 1999, became a minister and started his own ministry, Saving a Nation Endangered Church International, is just one example. Mase said then that he felt he couldn't serve what he called "two masters," hip-hop and God. His important story is chronicled in the autobiographical *Revelations: There's a Light After the Lime*. At that time, for him, these worlds were in conflict.

Since then, both the hip-hop world and the Christian world seem to be coming to the realization that the Christian hip-hop kid and the traditional Christian are both God's children inhabiting the same world. Rev Run, formerly of Run-DMC fame, is back to making hip-hop music with his recent release *Distortion*. Last year, Kurtis Blow, now an aspiring minister, announced that he was bringing his turntables into two Harlem churches, Abyssinian Baptist Church and Greater Hood Memorial A.M.E. Zion Church, a far cry from his early '80s hip-hop fame. Also in 2004, Kanye West rapped "Jesus Walks," a mainstream hit that reveals all of the inherent contradictions posed by Christianity and hip-hop. That year Mase too released another hip-hop album, *Welcome Back.* But leaving the church wasn't a prerequisite. Many may see these efforts and Mase's return to making hip-hop as hypocritical. In fact, each of these new efforts may be moving us closer to where we all need to be when it comes to the question of hip-hop and Christianity.

Both the black church and Christian hip-hoppers need to do more to make sense of the seeming conflicts between these two worlds. At least Efrem Smith and Phil Jackson think so. They offer hard questions to today's church leaders: If hip-hop brings people to have faith, makes youth come to church who previously didn't want to go, and helps hip-hop kids nurture a relationship with God, then why not? If we can go among prisoners and prostitutes to save souls, then what makes today's hip-hop youth so irredeemable? These are the difficult questions that Pastors Efrem Smith and Phil Jackson take on in this bold book.

The Hip-Hop Church is a practical guide that explores hip-hop roots and evaluates its potential to reach youth where they are: the hip-hop world. It's a complex world, and Smith and Jackson correctly identify hip-hop as the culture of this generation of youth, a culture that pervades their lives both as popular culture and as local, everyday lived culture. Beyond deciphering this brave new world for hip-hop outsiders, they offer traditional Christians seeking to build alliances with hip-hop kids very useful ways to access their world—from engaging youth in spoken word and activism to developing programming that taps into hip-hop's entrepreneurial spirit and its arts, such as break dancing. Equally important, they offer how-to suggestions for incorporating hip-hop into the church.

Part of the power of this long overdue book is that both pastors have themselves been to the territory. Not only have they grown up on hip-hop, as hip-hop generationers they are ministers who struggle with tradition and the challenges presented by a new generation via hip-hop culture. Phil Jackson and Efrem Smith recount the pitfalls and triumphs they've experienced trying to bring aspects of hip-hop into their churches. By offering insights into hip-hop culture and similarities between hip-hop and the black church, and by presenting actual sermons that incorporate the messages and lyrics of hip-hop, they've fired an important salvo into the Christianity/hip-hop debate.

In documenting hip-hop's impact over the last decade, I've written elsewhere that if hip-hop is indeed a culture—and it is—then it must have an economic philosophy, a political philosophy and a spiritual philosophy. With hip-hop now a multibillion-dollar business, countless artists like Master P and Jay-Z, who have risen from poverty to multimillionaire status, demonstrating its entrepreneurial spirit, have helped reveal its economic philosophy. We've seen the political philosophy in the way lyrics of Chuck D in the 1990s and, more recently, of Dead Prez and Immortal Technique have evolved into organizations like Russell Simons Hip-Hop Summit Action Network, The National Hip-Hop Political Convention and the League of Pissed Off Voters. The early result of this political philosophy can be measured in the Associated Press exit polls, which showed that over 4 million additional eighteen- to twenty-nine-year-olds voted in 2004 compared to the number in the same age group who voted in the 2000 presidential election.

Now it's time to see hip-hop's spiritual philosophy. With *The Hip-Hop Church,* Efrem Smith and Phil Jackson have initiated the important task of pointing us in the right direction.

Bakari Kitwana
Speaker, Professor and Author of *The Hip Hop Generation* and *Why White Kids Love Hip Hop*

FOREWORD

I am not a member of the hip-hop generation. I cannot rap. I cannot scratch. I cannot deejay. I cannot emcee. I cannot flow. I am, however, one who believes deeply in and am inspired by the hip-hop generation.

I am a member of the "soul" generation, offspring of those spirituals and blues and gospel and R&B and jazz children hewed out of hard living down in the Mississippi Delta, the Louisiana Bayou, the low country of South Carolina and Georgia, the Black Belt Prairie of Alabama and more, who migrated to Chicago, Detroit, New York and D.C. and to all points east and west. I am the transmission of ancestral memory. I am the premonition of hip-hop.

The soul children came of age during the era of Civil Rights and Black Consciousness, a time of well publicized black resistance and protest. The spirit of God was everywhere and made manifest in our music, our people, our worship, our very lives. The leadership of Martin Luther King Jr., Malcolm X, Fannie Lou Hamer, Rosa Parks, Angela Davis, Ella Baker, Kwame Nkrumah and Jomo Kenyatta empowered us. The poetry of Sonia Sanchez, Gwendolyn Brooks, June Jordan, Nikki Giovanni and Amiri Baraka inspired us. The sounds of James Brown, Aretha Franklin, Nina Simone, the Impressions, the O'Jays, Marvin Gaye, Stevie Wonder, Bernice Johnson Reagon, Gill Scott-Heron and the Last Poets moved us. To these leadings and promptings and more I listened and learned and danced—and prayed.

The same divine presence that was at work forty years ago is no less evident today in hip-hop music and culture. Regrettably, not everyone agrees with this assessment. Now more than ever, the great divides of race, gender, sexuality and class seem to fall along the fault line of intergenerational misgivings and distrust. This is most certainly true for Americans of African descent. All too often the civil rights generation is ready to decry the amnesia and irresponsibility of the hip-hop generation. With equal eloquence and defiance, the hip-hop generation trumpets the death of all civil rights sensibilities. Somewhere between these oppositional truths lies the much-needed recognition that we as a people are only as strong as our weakest link. Simply stated, we need each other.

Civil rights is black America's sacred legacy. Hip-hop is this era's sacred hope.

A number of social realities define the world of the hip-hop generation, from globalization and resegregation in the public sphere to deradicalization and commercialization in the churches. Despite what some have said, today's young people are no less spiritual than their predecessors, but they live in a time when the loss of faith in social institutions—no less religious ones—is understandable and epidemic. Many hip-hop heads speak truth to power saying, "I'm spiritual but I'm not religious." Theirs is the passionate quest for something deeper and more authentic than what often passes for religion.

If the black church would serve the present age it requires a greater commitment to social struggle and a deeper dedication to its own. Questionable theology, dubious politics, hierarchical practices, excessive materialism and an utter captivity to custom are the hallmark of many black churches in the twenty-first century. Hip-hop had to be born because, among other reasons, the black church was no longer being faithful to its own calling.

The black church and hip-hop are the two greatest repositories of our culture. Flawed messengers convey right and exacting messages in both. Flawed adherents immerse themselves fully in the experiences of both. The time is right for the two to be joined where coexistence is possible and betrayal is not to be had. Here and there across the land in urban, suburban and rural contexts the spoken word is indeed going forth. The gospel ministries and work artfully described in this volume by Efrem Smith and Phil Jackson, who pastor hip-hop churches in the Twin Cities (also my home) and Chicago respectively, are successful, exciting and real. In preaching, music, worship, counseling, social analysis and more these congregations offer vibrant insights that may transform the values, beliefs and traditions of hip-hop America—and enrich us all. The dominant message of hip-hop—of speaking your own mind and breaking down barriers—has long and variously been proclaimed by Grandmaster Flash and the Furious Five, KRS-ONE, Biggie, Tupac, Queen Latifah, Rakim, Lauryn Hill, Mary J. Blige, Jill Scott, Anthony Hamilton and Kanye West, just to name a few. For the hip-hop church movement, at the center of this message, always and without question, there is Jesus.

What these two churches have done, other churches can do. Strategies for effective outreach and ministry are found throughout the text. This work is pioneering and it is empowering, it is contextual and it is caring. Here is to a new movement in black and multiracial America—the hip-hop church—keepin' it real and keepin' it right.

Alton B. Pollard III, Ph.D.
Director, The Program of Black Church Studies and Associate Professor of Religion and Culture, Candler School of Theology, and Chair, American Religious Cultures Graduate Division of Religion, Emory University

SHOUT-OUTS

Phil

To my wife, whom I love and will love three days past forever. You are my air, and without you there would be no me! I thank God for you in my life, Kim.

To my two beautiful daughters, whom I am crazy about for life. You both are the light of my life.

To my one and only son, whom I love and am so proud of. You are my inspiration, and I am grateful to God that he has blessed me to be your father.

To my momma, who is the true definition of courage, hope, strength and encouragement! You are the motivator.

My sister, you are my laughter, my joy and my tender warrior.

To everyone at "The House" Covenant Church who keeps putting it down for Christ on the west side of Chicago. Thank you for dreaming in hip-hop context so that Christ is glorified and Satan is horrified. Continue to know him while we make him known, and I'll be there in a minute!

Love to Rev. Dr. Charles Briscoe and Rev. Honorable Dr. Emmanuel Cleaver. Thank you for your leadership.

To my pastor, Wayne Gordan. Thank you for the hope that pours out of you. This has been a cornerstone in my life and in our relationship. I love you man!

To my friends, accountability partners, colleagues in ministry and every student and young adult who I've ever worked with.

Finally, to all who love hip-hop and realize, as The Tonic put it, that "hip-hop blood types are not the same." Remember, if this is of Christ, it will last, but if it is of man, then it will fade away, so tell cats to stop hate'n and let God do his thing. For all the emcees, deejays, B-girls and B-boys, and taggers impacting the culture for Christ, keep representing him to the fullest.

Efrem

To Forice and Sandra Smith (Mom and Dad) for raising me in the church and in hip-hop.

To Elwood and Betty Jones for creating a hip-hop, go-go praise and worship experience.

To Fred and D'Ann Lynch, Stacey and Tryenyse Jones, Darius, Courtney and Julian for living out hip-hop as ministry.

To Sherrie Jones and Troy Williams for leading hip-hop and soulful worship at The Sanctuary Covenant Church.

To Donecia, Jaeda and Mireya (my family) for loving this hip-hop preacher.

Hip-Hop AND THE CHURCH
Opposition or Opportunity?

Sunday morning in Minneapolis: The auditorium of Patrick Henry High School in North Minneapolis reverberates with hip-hop beats. The Sanctuary Covenant Church is a growing multi-cultural church of over six hundred children, youth and adults, and this urban church is engaging the emerging generation through its distinctive approach to worship. Today is Hip-Hop Sunday, featuring four local Holy Hip-Hop groups, break dancing and spoken word.

During the praise and worship, Christian rap artists take turns leading the congregation in hip-hop praise. "When I say Jesus, you say Christ" starts the call and response between the rapping worship leader and the congregation. The youth and young adults rise from their seats and surge toward the stage with their hands up. One young man break dances, using his whole body to give God glory.

After the praise and worship ends, two youth recite a spoken word piece, "Inner City Blues," dealing with the recent shooting of a young man at a neighborhood restaurant in broad daylight. They cry out for a community that can find alternatives beyond violence to solve conflict.

The sermon, titled "Rules of Engagement," is based on the account of the apostle Paul's visit to Athens in Acts 17 and calls on the church to reach those living in hip-hop culture. During the sermon a deejay plays instrumental hip-hop beats to the rhythm of the black preaching art form.

This Sunday morning, a young African American man and a young European American woman give their lives to Christ, and others approach the altar committing themselves to reach those living in hip-hop culture for Jesus.

This is the church's first Hip-Hop Sunday, and plans are now in place for this special worship experience to happen six times a year. Though the Sanctuary Covenant Church has a contemporary, soulful flavor to its worship week by week, putting together a hip-hop service has been a stretch for this congregation. But the lives that have been transformed as elements of hip-hop have been incorporated into the worship experience make it all worthwhile.

Saturday night in Chicago: A long line of young people wait to get inside Lawndale Community Church, home of the first youth and young adult hip-hop church in the Midwest, known as The House. The topic tonight is sex. The flyers promoting the service looked like condom wrappers and had been placed in local music stores and other hang-out places of the hip-hop crowd.

This packed-out evening service features local Holy Hip-Hop emcees, videos on multiple screens, information on the outcomes of promiscuous sex, and drama. The night ends with a sermon calling attention to the Bible's teachings on sex. Lives are changed, commitments are made.

Many of the teens in attendance wish this service happened more than just twice a month. Such services are followed up, though, with Bible studies that take place daily all over the west side of Chicago, where youth and young adults can grow in the knowledge of God, with communication at a level they can truly understand.

✝

These vignettes are previews of what the book you are about to dive into is all about. We will wrestle with what it looks like for the church not only to engage hip-hop culture but to use elements within it as means for bringing the message of Jesus Christ to those living in hip-hop. Both of us are pastors who have grown up in the church and in hip-hop.

A WORD FROM EFREM: GROWING UP IN HIP-HOP

Though I am now the senior pastor of the Sanctuary Covenant Church in Minneapolis, I consider myself a hip-hopper as well. I grew up on hip-hop and in the church. I was born in 1969, and Bakari Kitwana in *The Hip Hop Generation* says the birth years of hip-hop were between 1965 and 1984. So in some ways I was raised by hip-hop. I remember the first smash rap hit, "Rapper's Delight," like it was yesterday. I was only a fifth-grader when the song hit the charts in 1979. One of my favorite lines in the song is this: "You ever been over your friends' house to eat / the food just ain't no good / the macaroni's soggy the peas all mushed / and the chicken taste like wood."

My journey and upbringing in hip-hop thus began with rap music. I began to get into artists and groups such as L.L. Cool J., Whodini, Run-DMC, Soul Sonic Force, UTFO, Eric B. and Rakim. Some of my favorite songs were "Funky Beat," "Five Minutes of Funk," "Roxanne Roxanne," "It's Like That," "I Need Love" and "Planet Rock." I grew up on Prince, Midnight Star, Cameo, Luther Vandross and New Edition mixed with Heavy D., 3rd Bass, KRS-ONE and M.C. Lyte in the same way that I grew up on collard greens, sweet potatoes, peach cobbler and catfish.

When I entered middle school my parents allowed me to start going to parties, and thereafter hip-hop captured me even more, not just as a music form but as a culture and community. Whether at Folwell Junior High School or at Martin Luther King Center, the party became my introduction to the elements of hip-hop. A series of movies called *House Party,* starring the rap duo Kid and Play, that came out during my high school years really captured my experience of the hip-hop party.

At the hip-hop party you see the deejay, whose job it is to "rock the party right" and keep people on the dance floor to the break of dawn (unless you had parents like mine who made you come home by midnight if not earlier). There was also the emcee, who would grab the microphone next to the deejay setup and rap lyrics of popular songs, showing creativity and great imagination. I will never forget Victor, a classmate of mine who was an awesome emcee. I don't understand why he didn't get a record contract. He rapped at talent shows, at parties and even in the hallway in between classes, battling others at our school on a regular basis. Then there were the break dance crews, breaking and pop locking; the rest of us would form a circle around them as various crews battled in dance with the same intensity as emcees battling in creative lyrics.

As I entered college, my taste in rap began to change as the genre itself began to change and expand. Consciousness—a more political and Afrocentric rap—came on the scene through groups like Public Enemy, X-Clan and Last Asiatic Disciples. Those hip-hop groups connected me to a deeper understanding of my culture and heritage.

So I grew up on hip-hop. When I didn't understand why my parents wouldn't let me go certain places and made me stay home while all my friends were out partying, hip-hop was there. When I starting dating girls, hip-hop was there. When I was feeling depressed, hip-hop was there. When I graduated from high school, hip-hop was there. When I graduated from college and moved into my first apartment, there was hip-hop. Hip-hop has always been around me in one way or another.

I was raised up in the African American church and in an urban multiethnic church on the tail end of the civil rights movement and the beginning of the great American experiment known as integration, brought on by the passing of both the Civil Rights Act and the Voting Rights Act. To put this all together, I grew up in a black church, hip-hop, integrated, increasingly multicultural world. I also grew up in an increasingly fast-paced, high-tech world. Sometimes my hip-hop life and my church life have intersected one another, other times they've seemed like two totally different worlds, and sometimes they've seemed like bitter enemies.

A WORD FROM PHIL: WHEN I CONNECTED TO HIP-HOP

Hip-hop is a way of life, an attitude, a strength that comes when the emcee, the deejay or even the tagger (graffiti artist) connects with you to say, "I understand, I feel where you are at." Hip-hop really spoke to several points in my life, but it wasn't until a friend died that I became deeply connected to the culture of hip-hop.

We sat in the parking lot of the funeral home as one of our friends was being hauled off on a hearse. There I was in my boy's ride, drinking and listening to "The Message" by Grandmaster Flash and the Furious Five. Mellie Mel dropped the hook: "Don't push me cause I'm close to the edge / I'm trying not to lose my head / a huh huh huh, huh huh / it's like a jungle sometime / it makes me wonder how I keep from going under."

We sat quietly, drank and meditated on "The Message." In some weird way, almost like a Negro spiritual sung by a soloist at church, the song brought us relief as we tried to deal with all the pain we felt.

That was when I knew that hip-hop had found its home in my life;

it spoke to my pain, my struggle as a young man seeking to find his way in the hood. This music was to me what Negro spirituals were to the church mothers of Jamison Temple CME Zion church in Kansas City, Missouri. Through hip-hop I was able to find myself and negotiate the issues of life in the city and realize at the same time that my situation was not helpless, that I was more than the shoes I could not afford or the gear I could not have.

What is so crazy about this feeling is that I never really knew that I needed this comfort in music, but when it hit me I knew I felt complete. This was the start of a marriage with hip-hop that would help me find myself, lose myself and find it again. I needed someone to hear my cry as a young boy growing up in the city; even though I went to church with my parents every Sunday, the church didn't hear me. I listened to my parents like kids do, but it was hip-hop that fed my soul. Rap as an element of hip-hop was the first way I was introduced to hip-hop, but what really engaged me to hip-hop was breaking and popping. I used to hit every park party, every house party and any club party I could find just to get with my little crew and pop. We would practice and then put it to work.

This element of hip-hop brought me more into the culture as I experienced it's impact on my life. What is great about the culture of hip-hop is that you don't have to rap, dance, tag or deejay; you just have to be.

It is in this *being* that God has called me to extract the components of hip-hop. Like Saul who met Christ on the Damascus road and whose message Christ flipped, using this wicked man to bring people to the kingdom, this is my passion and calling from inside the hip-hop culture. How can anything good come out of hip-hop to be used for the kingdom of God? Take some time, remove your prejudices or even misconceptions, and examine what God is doing through hip-hop in the church.

EFREM: CONNECTING HIP-HOP AND THE CHURCH

In November 2004, Oakcliff Bible Fellowship in Dallas hosted a summit that carried the title "Hip Hop and the Church: Collision, Compromise or Co-exist?" The purpose of this event seemed to be to connect parents to hip-hop as a culture, equip youth to think more critically about the types of rap music they listen to, and expose both groups to Holy Hip-Hop culture and music.

Such an event raises a lot of questions. Would bringing hip-hop into the church merely create a *collision* with churched adults who believe that this is just "worldly" music that is sending kids to hell? Are those in the church who advocate engaging with hip-hop culture and even creating a Holy Hip-Hop culture *compromising* the gospel of Jesus Christ? Can a hip-hop culture and Christianity *co-exist,* so that hip-hop actually becomes a relevant ministry? These are some of the questions this books seeks to wrestle with and even answer.

Collision. Are the church and hip-hop on a collision course, as both battle for the hearts and minds of young unchurched people within hip-hop culture? This position sees hip-hop as rap music that is corrupting our youth. The two are thus in a battle for young people—and it seems that rap music is winning:

> A further indication of what they deem a withering sense of values and social responsibility among the younger generation, they say, is the steady drop in youth membership and attendance in the Black church—long a community haven of spiritual centeredness and respectable values. According to the National Opinion Research Center at the University of Chicago, attendance for eighteen to thirty-five year olds has dropped 5.6 percent from 1995 to 2000.
>
> (BAKARI KITWANA, *THE HIP HOP GENERATION,* P. 22)

No doubt about it, hip-hop is a major influence among youth

and young adults today. Unfortunately, the collision position pits rap music against the church, where the church might rather seek to engage hip-hop as a culture for a kingdom purpose. The collision position on the church and hip-hop works only if you see the church as good and hip-hop as evil rap music, the church as godly and hip-hop as worldly. Then if the church attempts to hip-hop in any way, it is using things of the world, and in a collision theology it is wrong to use the things of the world to advance God's kingdom. This is not the perspective of all Christians, but some Christians take this position, pitting the church in opposition to hip-hop.

Julian writes in his song "Hip-Hop It Don't Stop" on his *Fruit of the Spirit* CD: "There's a faction whose reaction is to condemn using hip-hop music to win souls / for Him / Haters who can't seem to think outside the box, / Whose thoughts and minds are held shut with padlocks / Not realizing the impact that hip-hop has on the youth and young of today."

This book will explore hip-hop as more than just music, treating it as a culture that has a history as well as founding principles. Because of its significant influence, we believe hip-hop culture must be engaged by the church.

Compromise. Is it compromising the good news, the gospel of Jesus Christ, for the church to use hip-hop elements as tools for evangelism and discipleship? When gospel artists such as Kirk Franklin or Hezekiah Walker use the work of mainstream hip-hop artists such as R. Kelly or Sean "Puffy" Combs, are they compromising their mission? Is it okay to take a "secular" instrumental track and put Christian lyrics to it? Can your home music collection contain both Cross Movement and Mos Def? These are all questions that must be wrestled with when tackling the compromise question.

In some ways the collision position and the compromise position are practically the same. But it is possible for one to not see the church and hip-hop as being at war but still consider that there is no need for the church to use elements of hip-hop culture for ministry purposes. There may be many in the church who feel that incorporating any elements of hip-hop culture into the church's ministry would mean compromising its mission or its biblical principles. This book, however, will present a theology for engaging hip-hop culture as well as explore the movement known as Holy Hip-Hop.

Coexistence. By now you have probably guessed that coexistence is the position that will be explored in depth in this book. As pastors, we lead churches that use elements of hip-hop not only in the worship experience but also as outreach tools. The coexistence position sees hip-hop not just as music but as a culture, a milieu in which we are living and growing up. Hip-hop culture can be used as a vehicle to express the good news in a relevant way to the current generation.

Using elements of the culture we live in to proclaim the good news of Jesus Christ is not a new approach; the apostle Paul and Jesus himself did the same. Examining Scripture with care, we will seek to develop a theology of church and culture and also present ministry models that use elements of hip-hop culture to engage those who have been influenced by it. We will look at how, as Christian hip-hop artist Fred Lynch says, one of the most influential cultural forces today can be "spiritually hijacked" for purposes of building God's kingdom here on earth—especially in our urban centers, where youth and their families face many difficult barriers and challenges. This perspective should be taken under serious consideration especially in the African American church, which has a history of being focused on both evangelism and social justice.

USING THIS BOOK WHEREVER YOU ARE

Because hip-hop is a major influence in our world today, it's likely that several different kinds of readers will pick up this book. That's why we have divided the book into three major parts. Part one, "Why Should the Church Care About Hip-Hop?" encompasses one chapter that explores commonalities between hip-hop and the black church. In the African American church there should be a passion for those living in hip-hop culture, given its roots in the African American community as well as its connection to social justice. Because hip-hop is a movement rooted in the urban context but has influence beyond it, leaders of churches outside the city can glean from this section as well. This first section makes a biblical and theological case for why the church should engage hip-hop culture. Drawing from Scripture, a theology of church and culture is presented and is specifically applied to hip-hop culture. This section also considers those living in hip-hop culture and calls the church to develop a heart for them.

However, if you are outside of both the African American and urban contexts, you may want to jump right into part two, dealing with hip-hop as a postmodern cultural influence. Part two, "Understanding the Hip-Hop Culture," is designed for those who need to understand hip-hop as a culture, its elements and founding principles, its historical influence and even its spirituality. If your ministry is not in an urban area but you are in relationship with youth who are influenced by hip-hop and you want a greater understanding of it, this section will be helpful. If you're an older adult in an ethnic-specific urban setting and to you hip-hop is just rap and unintelligible noise, again this section is a great starting point.

Part three, "Bringing Hip-Hop into Your Church," presents Holy Hip-Hop as its own culture bringing the gospel of Jesus Christ to hip-hoppers—those living in hip-hop culture. Hip-hop ministry models are explored in order to encourage further development of hip-hop churches and youth-targeted hip-hop ministries within existing churches. If you are already knowledgeable of hip-hop culture and are ready to incorporate hip-hop ministry into your church or are feeling the call to plant a hip-hop church, feel free to jump right to part three and the resource section that follows.

Not every church will or should become a hip-hop church, but that is not really the point. The point is to move the African American urban church further along in its heart for unchurched youth and young adults growing up in hip-hop culture. The point is also to provide insight and tools for churches outside the African American urban context to engage youth who are influenced by hip-hop. Wherever you are, we want to connect you with the movement of hip-hop for ministry purposes, that together we may advance the kingdom of God among today's generation of youth and young adults.

Part One

WHY SHOULD THE CHURCH CARE ABOUT *Hip-Hop*?

1

CHURCH AND Hip-Hop

PHIL: NO ROOM FOR HIP-HOP?

Hip-hop is here to stay! I am a follower of Christ and I am hip-hop at the same time. I am hip-hop in my conversations, thinking, approach to faith, in my exegesis of Scripture, my homiletical style and how I relate to others; it is who I am and how I flow.

At one time, as a youth pastor, I taught that secular rap was against God's will and purpose and that believers should find their music only in Christian bookstores. We challenged our youth to confess their sin, live holy and throw away all the music that was not of God. One day I even held a service to which students could come and drop off all their music. The day came and we were ready with boxes—and the youth came and filled up a couple of them.

A couple of days later we went to a week-long Kids Across America Camp with these same students, some fifty in all. It was not until we came back from camp that I learned my own lesson about how God changes the hearts of people. After we arrived home and all the students had been picked up, about twenty of the kids I just had been with at camp came to my house. I opened the door, and there they all stood with smiles on their faces—and lugging big grocery bags and suitcases bulging with broken-up CDs, videos and cassettes (if you're old school, you know what I mean).

One of the student leaders said to me, "Phil, earlier we turned in some stuff, and some stuff we didn't turn in. But at camp God the Holy Spirit convinced us to be true to our commitment to get rid of this music, as it was hindering our walk." They went on to say that the first time they had turned in some music they were really trying to please me, but there was no conviction.

The lesson I learned from the Lord on that day was that *he* changes hearts—I must be faithful to exalt him and teach about him and his ways, and he will do the rest. I learned on that day that I must teach Christ crucified as a lifestyle and not as an addition to anything else. As Christ is lifted up and love for him is cultivated, our appetite to serve and live for him will become unquenchable, and nothing will stand in the way of this hunger. But when we give students lots of rules and regulations, what to do and not to do, they will be prone to seek to follow them and assume they are holy—and miss the greater holiness of love.

This is the bottom line: discipleship is a journey, not a destination. Along the way as I have encouraged and modeled the love of Christ to high school and college students, I have found there is something powerful in not seeking to control every component of a student's relationship with Christ. Rather, it is a matter of watching as the Holy Spirit brings about a sustainable faith in the student's life.

The pages to follow are birthed out of these ministry experiences. They invite you to understand hip-hop and the needs it meets in our culture and to let your thinking about rap and hip-hop be challenged.

EFREM: A SUMMIT ON HIP-HOP AND CHURCH

In the introduction I made mention of a 2004 summit held at Oakcliff Bible Fellowship in Dallas: "Hip Hop and the Church: Collision, Compromise or Co-exist?" The event was organized by Marcus "Goody" Goodloe, Oakcliff's youth pastor at the time. When he first invited me to participate, I didn't realize the magnitude of this summit; it proved to be a national event. The panel I sat on to discuss issues of hip-hop and the church included William Branch, also known as the Ambassador of the Holy Hip-Hop group and urban ministry Cross Movement, based in Philadelphia; urban gospel recording artist Brent Jones, of Brent Jones and the T.P. Mobb; and youth ministers and other representatives from megachurches and historic African American-led churches, such as The Potter's House (Bishop T. D. Jakes, pastor) and Concord Baptist (led for many years by the late E. K. Bailey) in Dallas as well as Windsor Village United Methodist Church of Houston (Kirby John Caldwell, pastor), the largest United Methodist church in the country. The church gymnasium where the event was held was packed with youth and parents eager to discuss this topic.

During the panel discussion, many issues surrounding hip-hop and its various messages were discussed from the perspectives of youth, parents and church leaders. Questions were raised delving deep into the meaning of hip-hop culture and its implications for sex, drugs, fashion, theology, the generation gap and worship. Is it all right to listen to so-called secular hip-hop? Why do youth influenced by hip-hop dress the way they do? Can you listen to a song just for the beat and not the lyrics? Is it okay for Christian artists to record songs with "secular" artists? How does one live in the world without being of the world? Why did rap star Mase leave mainstream hip-hop after becoming a Christian and pastor, only to return a few years later—though during his so-called retirement he had spoken of rap music as being of the devil? I wish I could say that we came up with answers to all these questions that night, but actually we answered some, debated some and wrestled together with others.

A number of things came clear to me that night.

First, hip-hop remains very influential in the United States, especially among youth, regardless of ethnicity, race or place of residence.

Second, except for a few senior and youth pastors, the church in America, and possibly beyond it, seems to be living in denial about the depths of this influence on church-attending youth. Many in the church see hip-hop as "worldly" and not fit to be connected to the church in any meaningful way.

Third, many parents just don't know what to do with the influence of hip-hop on their kids, because there is much they don't understand about it. They seem unable to reach back to their own teenage years and connect dots to this generation.

Fourth, many youth themselves seem to be in denial around the influence and power of music—its ability to draw them in and affect their behavior. They fail to notice that its impact is often more directive than reflective. Many say they are listening to songs mainly for their beat, yet they have memorized the lyrics to most of the rap songs in heavy rotation on radio stations around the country. The ways they talk, dress and build their social life have been influenced to some degree by hip-hop.

Why do I say this with such certainty? It's because I myself grew up thinking I was just into hip-hop for the beats. Only later did I realize the influence hip-hop had on my dress, haircuts and slang. Even today, hip-hop influences my preaching, dress and slang. The pervasiveness of hip-hop is one reason Phil and I chose to write this book. Young people in hip-hop culture as well as their parents and ministers need to be savvy about its elements and influence, its directive and reflective impact—both good and bad—and its echoes of biblical teachings and Christian theology, which can be harnessed for ministry.

Those who see hip-hop as a tool of the enemy probably tend to see culture as a general enemy—part of the world that is dominated by "the prince of the air," Satan. Others who have a broader theological perspective, however, see culture and the world differently. They see the world and culture as having potential to be controlled by forces of evil but also as having potential to be beautiful and reflect God's glory and will.

Hip-hop culture formed outside the church and has been used for evil, worldly purposes: degrading women, glorifying drug and alcohol abuse and addiction, and elevating violence as the primary means for solving conflict. However, ultimately we can see everything as created by God for God's purposes and to be enjoyed by human beings and used for kingdom purposes. Our enemy has used hip-hop for evil, but we can "spiritually hijack" it for evangelism, discipleship, justice and missions.

Historically, hip-hop has incorporated some positive themes, including peace, love, community and having fun. It is built on elements of dance, rap and visual art. The question then becomes, can these principles and elements be connected in some meaningful way to biblical teachings? If so, can these connections lead us to the development of a theology or missiology of hip-hop culture? Hip-hop's history and core elements, linked to a theology that bridges reconciliation, social justice and evangelical conversion and to practical ways hip-hop can be used in the local church, will be explored in this book. By understanding the history and foundational elements of hip-hop, the church can develop ministry models for presenting the gospel of Jesus Christ to the hip-hop community and those influenced by hip-hop. Such models are already being developed in churches such as Crossover Community Church led by Pastor Tommy Kyllonen in Tampa Bay, Florida, and The House, led by my coauthor, Pastor Phil Jackson. Further, Holy Hip-Hop artists are seeking to make a difference for the kingdom through music projects, concert tours and conferences.

On that November evening in Dallas, as I sat in a car with William Branch, the Ambassador of Cross Movement, waiting to be driven to the hip-hop summit, we engaged in a wonderful dialogue about hip-hop and the church. We talked about mainstream hip-hop artists who rap about Jesus on one track of their album and turn around and degrade women and glorify drug addiction on the next. We talked about how a Holy Hip-Hop culture should be separate from such a "mainstream." We wrestled with issues of hip-hop and the church.

HIP-HOP WITHOUT CHURCH

Urban young people grow up facing many issues, barriers and challenges that have roots in the influences of hip-hop, advanced technology and multiculturalism. They live in a fast-paced, in-your-face, hip-hop, multicultural world. Is the Christian church in a position to reach out to this generation of young people, nurturing and empowering them to live godly lives within these cultural influences? Can a church that is still one of the most segregated institutions in America, that includes many declining mainline Protestant congregations and that in many cases is ignoring hip-hop truly compete with the cultural influences youth live in and present the gospel of Jesus Christ to them?

To go down the road of this book, you first have to recognize that hip-hop is a major cultural force and influence among young people regardless of race, demographic or religious background. You also have to entertain the possibility that certain elements of hip-hop culture actually have biblical foundations. This would then lead you to ask why the Christian church today either has abandoned some of these elements or has refused to use them to present the gospel to young people in a relevant way.

Adults also live in this hip-hop- and multiethnic-influenced world. Hip-hop culture is all over the place—movie soundtracks, marketing strategies, music award ceremonies, video games, professional sporting events and of course the radio. Some adults try to ignore hip-hop, but if they have children they are exposed to it by default. And adults too live in a fast-paced, high-tech world and feel a desperate need to nurture the soul. This is why Oprah Winfrey, Dr. Phil (not to be confused with the Phil who's writing this book with me) and Chicken Soup for the Soul books have become so popular. Is the church in a position to equip adults to navigate the waters of the major cultural influences swirling around them and their children?

The Gospels show us how Jesus regularly hung out with "the wrong crowd"—tax collectors, drunks and the like. If he were walking the earth today, maybe he would be hanging out in inner cities with rappers, deejays, dancers and graffiti artists. Kanye West, a "secular" hip-hop artist, nearly lost his life in a car accident but was spared; he believes that indeed Jesus walks with him: "To the hustlers, killers, murderers, drug dealers / even the strippers (Jesus walks for them). / To the victims of welfare / feel we living in hell here / hell yea (Jesus walks for them)" ("Jesus Walks," *The College Dropout,* 2004).

Back when I was growing up in Redeemer Missionary Baptist Church, during devotion service I often heard the deacons and church mothers singing, "Walk with me, Lord, walk with me . . ." I can't help but see the connection between hip-hop and the church! Could it be that some within the hip-hop community are crying out for some sense of God in the midst of their inner-city upbringing, false masculinity, bling-bling or quest to become a woman of power and purpose? As the church rethinks evangelism and outreach, it needs to consider well the influence and impact of, and maybe even its intimate connection with, hip-hop—and to revisit God's heart for the people living within hip-hop culture.

GROWING UP IN THE BLACK CHURCH

My earliest church experience was in the black church. As a kid, I joined Tabernacle Missionary Baptist Church with my mother and was baptized there. The music was loud and full of passion, and when the preacher was preaching the people in the pews shouted back responses of "Amen!" and "Go ahead and preach!" My mother sang in the choir along with my grandmother. We started going to this church mainly because the senior pastor, Stanley King, was known in town as a very powerful preacher.

I grew up in that church, and we stayed there until I was about fifteen. That church influenced my life as much as if not more than hip-hop did. I was influenced by the black preaching style with its "whooping" rhythm and call-and-response interaction with those listening. I was drawn to how black preaching connected biblical stories with contemporary issues of growing up African American and urban. I was influenced by black gospel music, especially through the singing of the choir. I was influenced by deacons leading devotion before the start of the main worship service, with songs that not only cried out to God but celebrated the power of a God who has made a way for our people throughout our struggle for freedom. I was influenced by women sitting in the second row wearing white on first Sundays, serving me in some ways as an extended family.

The black church historically has been a refuge for African Americans beleaguered by oppression and racism. Historically, the black church has birthed African American leaders and colleges and has been a place of community development and financial empowerment. Even today black churches across the country are doing economic and community development through storefront and strip-mall projects that provide a holistic approach to ministry providing not only Sunday morning worship but also healthcare, workforce development and education programs. At the hip-hop summit in Dallas, I was able to see firsthand how the black urban church is more than a Sunday morning worship center. Oakcliff Bible Fellowship, the host church, has its own school and seems to be very involved in inner-city Dallas on a number of fronts. Such outreach is a significant expression of black church culture—a theology and a sense of mission rooted in the Bible but also in the specific struggles of African Americans.

Another dimension of black church culture is found in the worship experience, involving gospel music and the gospel choir. Black preaching has developed a unique style as well. There are even what could be called Afrocentric styles of organizing the various auxiliaries of the black church, such as the usher board, deacons board, mothers board and Sunday school board. Attending a black church is truly a cultural experience, and growing up in the black church influenced me in powerful ways.

THE CHURCH AND HIP-HOP MEET

For some years, though, I must admit that I was in the church and being influenced by it mainly because my mother was making me attend. Given the choice, I would have stayed home with my dad and watched the Minnesota Vikings, my favorite football team.

One of the things that really gave me new motivation for attending Tabernacle Missionary Baptist Church was something that to this day I'm surprised even started happening in a black Baptist church with mostly older members with roots in southern states such as Alabama, Florida, Mississippi and Texas. In the early 1980s, Pastor King came up with an idea to reach out to youth already in the church and our unchurched friends: a youth party that would include food, hip-hop music and dancing in the fellowship hall! And I'm not talking about Christian hip-hop; I'm not sure that Christian hip-hop, as we know it today, even existed back then. Pastor King consulted some of us on what this party should look like and what kind of music we liked.

Soon Friday Night at Tabernacle was launched, and thereafter it was held once a month. My friends and I would come into the fellowship hall of Tabernacle, and there would be a deejay set up playing SugarHill Gang, Kurtis Blow and Soul Sonic Force *in a church!* Some of the deacons and members of the mothers board would be in the kitchen, making chicken dinners and serving soda. The fellowship hall would be packed with young people, dancing and having fun. Pastor King's thought was that if young people in the neighborhood were going to be out partying on a Friday night, it might as well be in the church! Today when I think back on Friday Night at Tabernacle, I am aware that Pastor King and others at the church were meeting us where we were in order to connect us to the kingdom of God.

HIP-HOP AND THE SAMARITANS

Some may be scandalized by Friday Night at Tabernacle: Why were they playing secular music in the church? How could they let young people dance, even slow dance, in the church to music that wasn't holy? I believe, though, that this youth outreach was like Jesus' sitting at the well with the Samaritan woman in the Gospel of John chapter 4: "And he had to pass through Samaria" (John 4:4). The Samaritans could not boast a pure Jewish ethnicity, and their customs, values and traditions set them apart culturally from the "pure" Jews. The Jews did not see them as being on the same level. They were seen as impure, as second-class citizens, so they were avoided like the plague. If you were a Jew, you didn't want to have even the shadow of a Samaritan crossing you. But Jesus went to this place that other religious people had avoided.

In some ways youth can feel like second-class citizens in the church, sitting in the back of the church while the adults "get their praise on." Church programs in many urban African American churches are geared toward paying, I mean *tithing,* adults, not young people. When youth are recognized, it is because they are serving in the youth choir, youth usher board or youth council—merely mimicking adults and their behavior in the church. I'm not saying that this setup in and of itself is bad, but it can keep youth from feeling that they have their own space and platform for expression within the church, coming from their own generational experience. Does this seem too harsh an evaluation of how the church treats youth? I hope you'll at least consider whether the church is ignoring or dismissing the hip-hop culture that many youth live in and identify with.

As church folk look at hip-hop culture, do they see it as the Jewish religious community of Jesus' day saw the Samaritans? There are some real parallels.

Now hip-hop does include a lot of things that Christians would rightly call impure and unholy. How should a faithful Christian respond to lyrics that degrade women and glorify illegal drug use? How about videos that mainly portray women as sexual eye candy for males? What about the vulgar language that is on just about every rap CD listed in the top ten on the music charts? One could make the case based on this alone that Christians should avoid hip-hop the way Jews avoided Samaria. There is a mainstream presentation of hip-hop through television rap video shows that prides itself on being as violent, sexual and degrading as possible, it seems. If this is the only kind of hip-hop that is known, it's understandable that churches react by preaching that hip-hop should be avoided.

Yet in the Scriptures Jesus goes to the places that the "church" of his day stayed away from. Jesus went to where the outcasts and the impure lived. Jesus didn't avoid a questionable culture: the Scriptures say he *had to* pass through the culture others avoided.

What does this say to the church today? I believe it says that the church can't avoid the cultural context that young people live in. The church cannot avoid the culture that now has global and intergenerational influence. The church cannot avoid the culture of the unchurched postmodern urban community. To avoid hip-hop, given its wide influence on young people, is in some ways avoiding the youth themselves and treating them as modern-day Samaritans. As today's Samaria, the hip-hop community might be appropriately called "Samerica."

At Tabernacle Missionary Baptist, Pastor King came into our world, explored our culture and decided to use it to give us a place of refuge and fun within the church. He came into our world in order to build a bridge for us to come into his. Pastor King felt led to "pass through" the youth culture and incorporate what he found into an outreach strategy. There would have been no Friday Night at Tabernacle if Pastor King had not passed through our world and observed that there was a need to move us up from second-class citizenship status in the church. He realized that we lived in an evolving hip-hop world and his coming into to that world would lead to a deeper connection between our generation and the church.

"So he came to a city of Samaria, called Sychar, near the parcel of ground that Jacob gave to his son Joseph; and Jacob's well was there. Jesus therefore, being wearied from his journey, was sitting thus by the well. It was about the sixth hour" (John 4:5-6). At the well, Jesus found a place that historically symbolized common ground between the Jews and Samaritans. The mention of Joseph and Jacob from the Old Testament points back to a time when the Jews and Samaritans were one people. The Samaritans as a distinct people group were the product of the Jews' intermingling with other nations, which is why the Samaritans weren't seen as pure Jews.

Pastor King used a hip-hop dance party as a "well ministry" model. At the well of the hip-hop outreach party, common ground could be found. Dancing is intergenerational within African American culture and crosses the divide between the so-called secular and sacred. Even though Pastor King's generation had not danced to hip-hop, their experience of dancing to James Brown or the Motown Sound gave them common ground with the young people in the church and surrounding community. Even praise dancing within the church was part of this common "well" or place where the generations could connect to each other.

"There came a woman of Samaria to draw water. Jesus said to her, 'Give Me a drink'" (John 4:7). Jesus sat down at the well knowing that he would meet a Samaritan, because this was a place within that society where one would come for a drink. The well was a natural place to come into contact with the persons Jesus was wanting to reach.

During my teen years, hip-hop was a well to which I went on a daily basis to "drink." If a pastor would come into my world and sit at the well of hip-hop, that pastor would be more likely to reach my peers and me than if he only stood behind the pulpit on Sunday morning waiting for parents to force us to come to church. Pastor King didn't have to go far from the church to sit at this well; he merely had to decide to engage hip-hop culture. By sitting with the youth already in his church and connecting with those in the surrounding community, he placed himself at the well of our generation.

When Jesus asks the Samaritan woman for a drink, not only is he engaging in dialogue with her but he removes himself from an obvious position of power. His request takes the woman by surprise, not only because he is a Jew but also because he is a man. It was utterly unexpected for a Jewish man to ask a favor of a Samaritan woman! Intrigued, she let him know of her surprise—and a remarkable conversation ensued.

By asking us about our music and tastes as he planned the youth hip-hop outreach party, Pastor King was asking for a drink of the cultural and musical water that we drank regularly. To begin an authentic dialogue, the church must be willing to ask for a drink from hip-hop culture. Approaching hip-hop primarily from a position of judgment will *not* lead to real dialogue. That was Jews' normal approach to a Samaritan: looking at them and going right to the place of judgment.

I've met many parents who have a hard time sitting at the well of hip-hop with their own kids because their limited view of what hip-hop is, as presented to them through MTV or BET, drives them to judgment. I can't say that I totally blame them for this. If all I knew about hip-hop were the songs that degrade women, I would do the same thing. To be honest, with certain aspects of hip-hop right now I have a hard time sitting at the well rather than sitting in the judgment seat. To take the position at the well that Jesus took, he must have seen something in the Samaritans that others could not.

"The Samaritan woman therefore said to Him, 'How is it that You, being a Jew, ask me for a drink since I am a Samaritan woman?' (For Jews have no dealing with Samaritans.) Jesus answered and said to her, 'If you knew the gift of God and who it is who says to you, Give Me a drink, you would have asked Him, and He would have given you living water'" (John 4:9-10). As a young person, I wasn't used to being asked by a pastor to talk about hip-hop culture in order to plan a hip-hop party in the church! This took me off guard, but if I had known his full intentions for drawing me into a dialogue about the well from which I drank, I would have realized that he truly represented the good news of Jesus Christ, of which I desperately needed to drink for true refreshment. My well of hip-hop was being used by Pastor King to draw me to a well of water that brings with it abundant life!

"Jesus answered and said to her, 'Everyone who drinks of this water shall thirst again; but whoever drinks of the water that I shall give him shall never thirst; but the water that I shall give him shall become in him a well of water springing up to eternal life'" (John 4:13-14). Connecting the church to the well of culture to which those outside the church go to daily for refreshment can create a place of common ground, by connecting elements that can be traced back to common roots. More important, it can allow comparisons between the well of cultural water and the well overflowing with water of abundant life.

The woman said to Him, "Sir give me this water, so I will not be thirsty, nor come all the way here to draw."

He said to her, "Go, call your husband and come here."

The woman answered and said, "I have no husband."

Jesus said to her, "You have well said, 'I have no husband'; for you have had five husbands, and the one whom you now have is not your husband; this you have said truly."

(JOHN 4:13-18)

The atmosphere created at the well leads to honest dialogue between Jesus and the Samaritan woman about the real issues of her life. Similarly, the well of the hip-hop outreach party can bring church adults, young people outside the church and youth inside the church into relationship and conversation in ways that could be difficult without the well. Having received a chicken dinner and a soda from an adult at a church hip-hop party, I found myself more comfortable than normal with talking about what was really going on in my life. At the party the church adults were free to not act as "churchy" as they might on a Sunday morning during service; here they could speak into my life in a way that would catch me off guard and draw me in.

From here on in John 4, Jesus connects the issues of the

woman's life to worship—a worship that will break down the walls of separation between Jews and Samaritans.

Jesus said to her, "Woman, believe Me, an hour is coming when neither in this mountain, nor in Jerusalem, shall you worship the Father. You worship that which you do not know; we worship that which we know, for salvation is from the Jews. But an hour is coming, and now is, when the true worshippers shall worship in spirit and truth; for such people the Father seeks to be His worshippers. God is spirit, and those who worship Him must worship in spirit and truth."

(JOHN 4:21-24)

I must admit that the type of hip-hop I listened to as a teen was leading me to worship something I truly didn't know, because I wasn't critically examining the well water that I was drinking on a daily basis. Through the hip-hop outreach party at Tabernacle, I soon made a transition to new water. My worship began to shift from music to the Creator of music and other art forms. Though I wouldn't truly understand what it meant to become and live as a Christian until after Tabernacle Missionary Baptist Church was no more, the experience I had there met me at the cultural well of my life and from there pointed me to new water and worship. My involvement in the hip-hop party connected me to loving adults in the church and led me to get involved in the church in numerous ways, so that the church came to be just as much mine as my mother's and grandmother's. For a time my growing up in hip-hop and the church connected in a powerful way. Until then I had tended to assume that I had to live two separate lives, one in the church and one in hip-hop, but Pastor King made a connection that I hadn't thought was possible. His ministry used my love of hip-hop to connect me in a deeper and richer way to the church and God.

Unfortunately, for reasons I never knew, after about a year the Friday night hip-hop party was discontinued. Soon after that Pastor King left as senior pastor of the church, and then the church was discontinued and a new church called Redeemer Missionary Baptist Church took its place. That church is still present in South Minneapolis today, but no hip-hop outreach parties are being held in that church building, as far as I know.

Today hip-hop is still very influential among youth and adults outside the church, yet developing ministry "wells" with those living within hip-hop is not all that common. Many church people would resist playing secular rap within the church or throwing dance parties in the fellowship hall. But there is still a need to sit at the well of hip-hop in order to build relationship, develop dialogue and offer the overflowing water of abundant life that is Jesus Christ.

The hip-hop ministry that was set up at Tabernacle Missionary Baptist Church was set up within the walls of the church. Today I believe the "well" of common ground between the church and hip-hop must be found both inside and outside the church. For this to happen on a larger scale, though, the church must have a theology of engaging culture, which then is worked out specifically in hip-hop culture.

MISSION SPREADS TO HIP-HOP CULTURE

When one begins to see hip-hop as more than just rap music, as a whole culture, new doors open for evangelism, and we can become learners, observers and missionaries to those living in hip-hop culture and those influenced by it. In our contemporary urban culture, we can be like Paul when he addressed the altars built to unknown gods in Athens and used them as vehicles to present the true God who can be known intimately through Christ Jesus.

"Now while Paul was waiting for them in Athens, his spirit was being provoked within him as he was beholding the city full of idols" (Acts 17:16). Paul noticed idolatry around him in the city of Athens. In similar fashion, hanging out in urban hip-hop culture raises its own issues of idolatry. When I read stories in hip-hop magazines about rap artists who can't record their songs without being high on weed and drunk on Jack Daniels, my spirit is provoked like Paul's was. Seeing videos with nearly naked women falling all over the male star provokes my spirit—that is another form of idolatry. There are aspects of hip-hop culture that grieve my spirit deeply as truly idolatrous practices are lifted up as just a normal way of life for the youth culture.

Here we must keep in mind, though, that this verse is not the end of Paul's response to the culture around him. And this should not be the verse that totally defines how the church responds to hip-hop culture—merely being provoked by the aspects of it that are degrading and idolatrous. We must continue with the text if we are to form a biblical theology of church and culture.

"So he was reasoning in the synagogue with the Jews and the God-fearing Gentiles, and in the marketplace every day with those who happened to be present" (Acts 17:17). Paul didn't wallow in his outrage at the idolatry in the culture around him. He set about reasoning with the people of Athens. In his ministry as laid out in Scripture, Paul had to deal with opposition from his fellow Jews as well as from other belief systems and philosophies within the various cultures he encountered as he traveled. He had to be able to reason with people of various religions and philosophies.

Does the church desire to follow Paul's example and reach out in a meaningful way to those living in hip-hop culture, a very influential movement among youth and young adults in our society? For me, the answer is yes! I desire to have fruitful conversations and reason with those in my community who are outside the church and immersed in hip-hop culture. I don't want to stop at handling the Word of God behind a pulpit and reasoning in the

church as Paul did in the synagogue; I also want to be able to reason and communicate effectively with those in the hip-hop-influenced urban community surrounding the offices of my church.
These are the contemporary artistic philosophers of urban culture.

And also some of the Epicurean and Stoic philosophers were
conversing with him. Some were saying, "What would this idle
babbler wish to say?" Others, "He seems to be a proclaimer
of strange deities," because he was preaching Jesus and the
resurrection.

And they took him and brought him to the Areopagus, saying, "May we know what this new teaching is which you are
proclaiming? For you are bringing some strange things to our
ears; we want to know therefore what these things mean."

(ACTS 17:18-20)

Paul was able to be real about how some aspects of the culture
troubled his spirit but still have dialogue with philosophers of the
culture. How must the church position itself in order to gain a
hearing and build relationships with those living in what I see as
the strongest expression of postmodern urban culture? This is the
question that African American and multiethnic urban churches
must wrestle with, along with churches outside urban areas.

Paul develops a relationship with the philosophers of the city of
Athens. There are philosophers within hip-hop culture too, and I
want to have dialogue with them. Preachers of the church and
philosophers of hip-hop ought to be in conversation.

By engaging with hip-hop culture as a pastor, I am subject to
the same diversity of responses as Paul received from the philosophers of the culture of the city of Athens. When I'm hanging out
with youth and young adults within hip-hop and urban street culture, I get many responses. Some look at me wondering what I'm
doing there, others are excited that I want to connect with them in

meaningful dialogue, and with some I get the chance to talk about my theology and compare it with their philosophy.

Sometimes I am a bit surprised by such responses; since I grew up in hip-hop, at times I wonder why my connection with folks in today's hip-hop culture isn't always automatic and easy. I have to remind myself that the older I get, if I don't stay in touch with urban youth culture I can become an outsider to it. I also have to remember that now that I'm a pastor, and whether I like it or not, I'm perceived as an outsider by hip-hoppers outside the church and even some who are in the church. My goal is to be a Christian hip-hop theologian within hip-hop culture, having dialogue and reasoning with hip-hop community members and philosophers.

To me, rappers are the greatest hip-hop philosophers within hip-hop culture. Their remarkable communication skills prepare them to be the philosophers of the culture. KRS-ONE is not only a pioneering emcee but also a philosopher of hip-hop, lecturing on college campuses all across the country. In his book *Ruminations* he explores hip-hop from philosophical, academic and theological perspectives. His book makes it clear that hip-hop is indeed more than music. In a foreword, radio and TV host Tavis Smiley compares this pioneering rapper to our great African American influencers: "In many ways, this book actually rests in the tradition of great thinkers like W. E. B. DuBois, Carter Woodsen, and John Henrik Clarke, men who have sought to develop a cultural veil through which to interpret the seeming insanity of America" (pp. 9-10). The book comes with a CD featuring lectures of KRS and contemporary African American intellectual and religious scholar Cornel West.

Those who think that hip-hop is purely negative, putting down women and glamorizing violent crime, will be surprised by KRS-ONE's chapters such as "The Science of Rap," "On Reparations and the Civilized State of African Americans" and "The Spiritual Meaning of 9-11." He begins the book with what is called the Overture:

And suddenly I realized the obvious truth! The world will not change unless I change it! For years I believed that the way in which I viewed the world was the way in which most people viewed the world. I believed that it was obvious to all thinking human beings that civilization should always preside over technology. That before you are a race, a religion, or an occupation, you are a human being. And that human rights demand human duties. That people should be governed by law, not by the agendas of the rich. That it was the responsibility of all Americans to reflect upon, continue, and honor the legacy of Bayard Rustin, Kwame Toure, Dr. Martin Luther King Jr., Malcom X, Marcus Garvey, Rev. Jesse Jackson, Dr. Cornel West, and Rev. Al Sharpton. I believed that devout Christians, Jews, Hindus, Muslims, etc., really valued their relationship with God. I believed that everyone wanted to be free. That no one enjoyed slavery and/or addiction. I believed that everyone saw things this way. However, to my surprise I was wrong! (PP. 15-16)

Man, would I love to reason with someone like that—but wait, I can! There are hip-hop philosophers and persons influenced by hip-hop culture all around me. I must ask myself if I have anything to say to them, any bridge to build to them.

The introduction to the book is called "Urban Inspirational Metaphysics," which he says "is all about unlearning" (p. 23). He speaks this as a program focusing on the "spiritual advancement of those that live within today's inner cities." The Christian church ought to want to be in relationship with a movement with a mission such as that.

Now, given that KRS-ONE is married to Pastor Simone G. Parker of Atlanta, he may have an issue with my portraying him as a philosopher more than a theologian, but I refer to him this way because *Ruminations* doesn't use an explicit biblical foundation as far as I read to develop and support its points. I don't lean on his writings to advance a theology of hip-hop ministry but to give an understanding of hip-hop being more than music. KRS-ONE is a legendary emcee, but in my opinion, not one who presents an orthodox Christian theology.

The main point is that hip-hop is a culture and within the culture there are philosophers. If the church wants to engage hip-hop culture, not just be provoked in spirit by its idolatrous negative side, it must build bridges with the culture so that theologians, church members and hip-hop philosophers might reason together.

So Paul stood in the midst of the Areopagus and said, "Men of Athens, I observe that you are very religious in all respects. For while I was passing through and examining the objects of your worship, I also found an altar with this inscription, 'TO AN UNKNOWN GOD.' Therefore what you worship in ignorance, this I proclaim to you. The God who made the world and all things in it, since He is Lord of heaven and earth, does not dwell in temples made with hands; nor is He served by human hands, as though He needed anything, since He Himself gives to all people life and breath and all things; . . . for in Him we live and move and exist, as even some of your own poets have said, 'For we also are His children.'"
(ACTS 17:22-25, 28)

By engaging the culture of Athens, Paul is able to gain an audience with them and reason with them. He uses an interesting strategy for proclaiming the message of the one true God: he refers to the Athenians' own altars and quotes one of their own poets. He starts out his presentation to the men of Athens by saying he has observed that they are very religious.

To engage hip-hop culture, we must observe it and study it. In order to influence the hip-hop culture with the gospel of Jesus Christ, we ought to know something about it. For an introduction to hip-hop, I suggest the Nelson George books *Hip Hop America* and *Post-Soul Nation*. Both of these books give the reader an understanding of hip-hop elements and history and its roots in African American urban culture. George provides what I consider the African American, hip-hop and urban take on postmodernism. Greg Tate speaks of this in a book he edited, *Everything but the Burden: What White People Are Taking from Black Culture.*

Nelson George once correctly identified the African-American equivalent of postmodernism as post-Soul culture. Soul music widely understood as the classic sound Black gospel vocalists like Sam Cooke made as they turned away from praising Jesus and toward the more lucrative romantic pop market, subsequently produced a secular faith of sorts—one built around the verities of working-class African-American life. Soul culture succinctly describes the folkways African Americans concocted in the desegregating America of the fifties and sixties as the civil rights movement was on the ascendancy. Post-Soul is how George describes the African-American culture that emerged out of the novel social, economic, and political circumstances the sixties Black movements produced in the wake. Post-Soul would include the plays of Ntozake Shange, the novels of Gayl Jones, the films of Spike Lee, the music of Fishbone, Tracy Chapman, and Living Colour, the presidential campaigns of Jesse Jackson, the songs and the cosmetic surgery of Michael Jackson, the art of Jean-Michel Basquiat, and of course that post-modern expression par excellence, hip-hop.

(INTRODUCTION, P. 6)

Observing and studying hip-hop culture, the church, especially the African American church, will learn something it badly needs to grasp: in this postsoul culture there is a widening gap between African American culture and the church. Further, there is a widening gap between the urban church and its surrounding community. Over the last thirty years, has the church truly noticed and observed the evolution of an urban culture that is spiritual but in many ways has defined itself outside the church and Christianity? The hip-hop culture has been evolving not only outside the church but also outside mainstream black political movements such as the civil rights movement. This hip-hop culture also presents within its evolution a generation gap as well. Pastor James White of North Carolina said during a radio interview with me, "For the first time there is a very visible generation gap in the African American community, and hip-hop culture has a lot to do with it." How many African Americans in the hip-hop generation has the church lost because it hasn't been paying attention to what going on in postsoul African American culture?

This is a major reason I believe youth ministry is a must in the African American urban church. The church must be prepared to engage a culture whose leaders and philosophers are teenagers and young adults. This may take a rethinking of not only theology but also approaches and methods of ministry.

As Paul addresses the men of Athens, he speaks of examining the objects of their worship. He is aware of the various altars of the culture of Athens because he has examined them. He quotes an inscription on one of the altars he examined to draw a direct connection to the God of the universe.

And as we engage with hip-hop culture, we begin to see what is worshiped within it. What do those in hip-hop and outside the church value? What do they believe is life giving? Do they value God? If so, which god?

There are various altars of worship within hip-hop. There is the altar of sensuality and sexuality outside of marriage. There is the altar of "bling-bling," with many creative and evolving ways to wear jewelry. There is the altar of pimped-out rides with rims. There is the altar of fashion. There is the altar of being the best emcee. There is an altar of spirituality in hip-hop as well. There are many altars within hip-hop.

It should be acknowledged too that Christian hip-hop artists are attempting to bring hip-hop to the throne room of the Lamb, Jesus the Christ. Their purpose is to generate an underground movement and develop a Holy Hip-Hop culture. I will deal with this in a later chapter.

Let's consider the elements and original principles of hip-hop as an altar of the culture. Could these elements and principles be used like the inscription Paul quoted from the altar in Athens, to draw a direct connection to the one true God of the universe today?

The original elements of hip-hop culture are the emcee, the deejay, graffiti art and the dance. There are parallel elements in the church, such as the preacher, the praise and worship leader or the choir director, visual art such as stained-glass windows, and praise dancing. In this book Phil and I won't be looking at all the elements of hip-hop culture in depth, but you will find chapters on both the emcee and the deejay, who can be compared to the preacher and the worship leader. By connecting elements of hip-hop to elements of the church, we may find common ground in order to reason together about the authenticity of Jesus the Christ.

KRS-ONE says that hip-hop was established as a community of peace, love, unity and having fun. Perhaps we could see this original purpose as an "inscription" on the founding altar of hip-hop culture and use it to proclaim the one true God.

Some Christian ministers shun hip-hop because of one of its founders, Afrika Bambaataa. Here is how Nelson George describes Bambaataa: "Growing up in the Bronx River Projects, Bambaataa became a member of one of the city's biggest youth gangs, the Black Spades. . . . In 1974, Bambaataa founded the Zulu Nation, a collective of DJ's, breakers, graffiti artists, and homeboys that filled the fraternal role gangs play in urban culture while de-emphasizing crime and fighting" (*Hip Hop America,* p. 18). Some in the church may look at Bambaataa's background and deem hip-hop secular and ungodly because of such origins. Bambaataa is not a professed Christian, and his Zulu Nation could be seen as a cult. But if we use the ministry model of Paul in Athens, we can look at the founding purposes of hip-hop—love, peace, unity and fun—and use them to proclaim Christ. Why give Bambaataa the credit for creating love and unity when God can be proclaimed as love and our unifier through his Son Jesus? By examining the altars of hip-hop culture, then, the church can develop ministry models for proclaiming the good news of Jesus Christ to the hip-hop community at a level it can truly understand and receive.

Finally, Paul quotes the poets of the Athens culture to proclaim truth. He is familiar enough with the poets of the day that he knows how to use the words of these poets, not the words of Jesus, to proclaim truth at a level the men of Athens can understand.

There has been controversy over the song "Jesus Walks" by Kanye West because of other songs in the same project that include vulgarities. But what about using the "Jesus Walks" lyrics to actually proclaim truth about the authentic Jesus to the hip-hop community? In an interview Kanye West has said that he didn't create the song for church folks. It's a shame that he recognizes an evangelistic purpose for the song while many Jesus followers do not.

Rappers are the poets of the hip-hop culture. We do well to examine rap for lyrics that can be used to proclaim truth back to the hip-hop community. A great example of this is the book *Jesus and the Hip-Hop Prophets,* where John Teter and Alex Gee show how lyrics from hip-hop artists Lauryn Hill and Tupac can be used as ministry tools.

From the account in Acts 17, then, we can draw a theology of church and culture that can be used today to show us why and how the church—especially African American and urban churches—should engage hip-hop culture. Hip-hop is a major influence among youth and young adults, so even if your ministry is not African American or urban, if you are responsible for ministering to youth, you should care about hip-hop. Fortunately, within the original elements and founding principles of hip-hop we can find connecting points we can use to build bridges from hip-hop culture to the church. Those of us in the church who have a passion for youth and others living in hip-hop culture must take advantage of this great opportunity.

Part Two

UNDERSTANDING THE
Hip-Hop CULTURE

2

WHAT IS Hip-Hop?

EFREM: I'M A MEMBER OF THE HIP-HOP NATION

Hip-hop is about dance, art, expression, pain, love, racism, sexism, broken families, hard times, the search for God and overcoming. Outsiders readily assume that hip-hop is just rap music, but that is because they are not aware of the history and the current impact and influence hip-hop has on the whole youth culture.

Born in 1969, I am a part of the hip-hop generation. I watched hip-hop evolve from underground house parties in the basements of my friends' houses to Run-DMC videos on cable television to the existence of rap millionaires like Sean "Puffy" Combs, Master P, Suge Knight and Russell Simmons. These rich African American men are more than just rappers; as a matter of fact Russell Simmons doesn't even rap. Simmons has been behind the scenes of hip-hop, developing it from rap artists and groups like Run-DMC, L.L. Cool J. and Kurtis Blow to films like *Krush Groove* and *Tougher Than Leather* and clothing lines like Phat Farm. A true pioneer of the culture, Simmons opened the door so that others in the movement could thrive—for example, so that Sean Combs could own his own Bad Boy record label and develop his own clothing line, Sean John. These innovators are the architects of culture, starting from the streets of the city and now influencing the suburbs and even small rural towns. They took the hustle of the street and turned it into a Wall Street economy.

If you are a youth worker, it doesn't matter whether you're in a church or a parachurch organization, city or suburb, or if your kids are Latino, Asian or Irish: hip-hop is influencing your situation. The kids you work with may not love hip-hop, but they're being influenced by it. If your kids wear oversized jeans with the tops of boxers showing, oversized athletic jerseys, tennis shoes such as Air Force Ones or long chains around their necks, that is hip-hop. When white girls go on a youth group trip and sit in the bus or van braiding their hair in the style of an Ethiopian queen, that's hip-hop. There are things around you daily that are constantly calling out, "Long live hip-hop!" If you truly want to understand the culture that youth live in today, it's important to understand hip-hop—as a culture, not just a music form.

Nelson George says this about the culture of hip-hop and its influence:

> Rap music, and hip hop style as a whole, has utterly broken through from its ghetto roots to assert a lasting influence on American clothing, magazine publishing, television, language, sexuality, and social policy as well as its obvious presence in records and movies. . . . Advertisers, magazines, MTV, fashion companies, beer and soft drink manufacturers, and multimedia conglomerates like Time-Warner have embraced hip-hop as a way to reach not just black young people, but all young people.
>
> (*HIP HOP AMERICA*, P. IX)

KRS-ONE's book *Ruminations,* mentioned in the previous chapter, explores hip-hop's connections to philosophy, religion, government and corporate America. He presents hip-hop as a commentary from "the hood," with rappers functioning as inner-city journalists who through their rap, dance and graffiti report on what's going on in the city and the world at large. Sometimes the reporting comes across with the soft melody of Marvin Gaye's "What's Going On?" from the Motown era. Sometimes the reporting is done with the pride of James Brown's "Say It Loud, I'm Black and I'm Proud." And there are other times when the reporting explodes with the anger of the Isley Brothers' "Fight the Power." Hip-hop is influenced in many ways by such R&B soul music; George refers to hip-hop as "post-Soul" culture. "Post-Soul" could be considered the urban take on *postmodernism,* a term used more often in white cultural circles to describe what's going on in the world around us (later in this book we will deal with hip-hop as urban postmodern culture). KRS-ONE describes hip-hop culture this way:

> True Hip-hop is a term that describes the independent collective consciousness of a specific group of inner-city people. Ever growing, it is commonly expressed through such elements as: Breakin' (dance), Emceein' (rap), Graffiti (aerosol art), Deejayin', Beatboxin', Street Fashion, Street Knowledge, and Street Entrepreneurialism. Discovered by Kool DJ Herc in the Bronx, New York around 1972, and established as a community of peace, love, unity, and having fun by Afrika Bambaataa through Zulu Nation in 1974, Hip-hop is an independent and unique community, an empowering behavior, and an international culture.
>
> (*RUMINATIONS,* PP. 179-80)

With its elements of the deejay, the emcee, dance, visual art, fashion, language and big business, hip-hop goes far beyond just a music form. It encompasses the culture of African Americans, Latinos and urban America more generally. When I was in middle school and high school, hip-hop was more than just music for me; it meant finally feeling like my voice was in the mainstream of American culture. Really it felt like the voice of urban youth culture, especially those of color, were finally in the mainstream.

Keep in mind that hip-hop evolved after the civil rights move-ment—which had young people on the front lines—brought for-malized and legalized integration. Hip-hop is not, of course, the first popular movement to use the arts to speak to political, social and spiritual issues, but it has done so representing the under-class of urban America as well as the African American middle class as it fights assimilation.

PHIL: UNDERSTANDING HIP-HOP

In order to understand the culture of hip-hop you have to under-stand youth culture, and in order to understand youth culture you have to understand urban America. Now I know that may sound like a shock to you, but it is reality. What affects the hood every day and becomes commonplace there becomes all the rave in the suburbs among middle- and upper-class white, black and Latino kids. Already when the first commercial hip-hop record came out, "Rapper's Delight" by the SugarHill Gang, 70 percent of the LPs were bought by white American teens! That is one reason it stayed on the *Billboard* list for over twelve weeks. This started the widespread influence of urban youth culture. The communities that had been dumped on—neglected and oppressed—for so long would now be influencing the kids of affluent suburban par-ents who were scared to death of what they saw on the ten o'clock news.

Why is it that the Asian kid would rather wear his pants baggy, hat cocked to the side and rocking a Wu-Tang Clan cut on his iPod? Why is it that the white girl from the Catholic prep school leaves a Missy Elliott cut blasting from her car in the parking lot after a basketball game? Maybe it's because it is a deeper con-nection between them than just the music; maybe there is an in-fluence that runs deeper than the entertainment of rap; maybe there is a connection that runs deeper than appearances.

That connect, that pull, is the culture of hip-hop. Over the last thirty to forty years, youth culture has shifted: where once there were moldable young people you could just tell what to do, there are now young people telling folk what they ain't gonna do! Where once there were young people who would just wait on justice to roll down whenever it would, there are now young people who want their voices heard and heard *now!* This group of young people, according to Bakari Kitwana, grew up between 1965 and 1985 (I believe the generation actually began one year prior), and grew up more media savvy and more impatient about suffering for the cause while nothing is being done about it.

The other day I was watching a rapper at an event. He was just going and going, and he was dropping some tight lyrics. As he walked off the stage, I noticed that his shirt bore an interesting message:

I HATE RAP
BUT I LOVE HIP-HOP

If you ask the average older adult on the street, "Why is hip-hop so important to this generation?" you will get one consistent reply: "Isn't hip-hop just rap music?" But if it is just rap, how could it sustain itself for so long and mean so much to so many people? Again, hip-hop is a subculture unto itself; rap is just one element within it that speaks into and combines with many others to create the subculture.

In an intro to his album *Black on Both Sides* (a classic hip-hop album, featuring real hip-hop rhyme and messaging styles), Mos Def says:

People always ask me, "Yo, Mos, what is happening with hip-hop?" I tell them, "Whatever is happening with us. If we smoked out, then hip-hop is going to be smoked out; if we are fine, then hip-hop is going to be fine. People be talking about hip-hop as if it is some type of giant sitting on the hillside. *We* are hip-hop! So the next time you wondering where hip-hop is going, ask yourself, "Where am *I* going? What am *I* doing?"

As Mos says, hip-hop is more than its elements. The hip-hop subculture manifests itself in people, and as people identify the needs in their life that hip-hop meets, the culture is sustained. To minimize hip-hop by saying it is just rap is to disrespect it, because hip-hop is life.

A few years ago *Vibe* magazine ran a great article chronicling the life of Biggie Smalls and Tupac. The writer wondered what the big deal was with these two rappers, how much of a legacy they have left for the world and how much they have impacted people. What it all boiled down to, he concluded, was that these two emcees made people "feel their existence most powerfully." That statement hit me like a ton of CDs. We in the ministry of Jesus Christ are called to create an atmosphere in which people encounter Christ Jesus so as to feel their existence most powerfully. How is it that we in the church, representing God, the Father of Jesus Christ, the Savior of the World, have missed it with this generation?

Hip-hop was birthed from the people, by people who were disenfranchised by the rest of the world. In his book *Can't Stop, Won't Stop: A History of the Hip-Hop Generation,* Jeff Chan gives insight into the social climate that gave birth to hip-hop. It all started in the Bronx, New York, in the 1950s when a cat named Robert Moses, one of the most significant urban builders of his time, was contracted by the city of New York to build the Cross-Bronx Expressway. During the big "urban renewal projects" in the 1950s and 1960s, many cities were building such expressways to allow people to move quickly from their suburban homes through the city and into downtown to shop. Well, in the Bronx as in a lot of other cities, these moves were profitable for some but disastrous for others. Jobs were displaced as middle-class residents moved to the suburbs; whole communities were gone. In New York, the Cross-Bronx Expressway caused the loss of over 600,000 manufacturing jobs; over 60,000 residents were affected.

In the 1970s poverty and joblessness were prevalent, gangs were infesting the community with drugs, and hopelessness was the way of life in the Bronx. By the mid-1970s the youth unemployment rate was at 60 percent, and the apartment buildings once managed by owners who were invested in the community were now left to slumlords. The slumlords soon developed a scam to get more money out of the system. For as little as fifty dollars, they would hire thugs and have them burn down an apartment building. Insurance policies then rewarded the conniving owner with $150,000 or more.

In less than a decade, some 43,000 housing units were burned down. Senator Daniel Patrick Moynihan, a New York Democrat, threw up his hands: "The people in the South Bronx don't want housing or they wouldn't burn it down." The "urban renewal" projects did little for the urban communities or the people living in them; rather, they generated an intense resistance to the system and anything resembling the system.

Hip-hop arose against the South Bronx's backdrop of poverty, tension over economic injustices, social injustice and social change. Music has always been the outlet by which a people expresses its struggles, and hip-hop is no different. The children, youth, young adults and older adults trying to raise families under difficult conditions have to be heard, and often the powers that be are not listening.

Artists rapping about various issues faced on the street sometimes seem offensive to others (who are not familiar with the street) when they talk about how they beat the system using its negative aspects. The slumlords, for example, saw a way to "get over on" an already corrupt system that almost forces them to become corrupt in order to survive. The average young person growing up in these conditions tends to develop a pattern of thinking in which hopelessness and resiliency coexist.

I grew up in the hood. While me and my boys were shooting dice on the corner, the OGs (Original Ganstas) would stop us and shout, "You ain't gonna be s*&$! You might as well drop out of school." They always questioned us about why we wanted to go to college—"we didn't go to college and look at us."

At the same time, school counselors frequently warned kids with good grade-point averages that they should not apply to bigger universities because they would not get in; they should just plan to go to the junior college. Gradually we started to think and believe, *We ain't gonna make it off the block, so what are we studying and trying to go against the tide for?* We became stronger—more resilient—in hopelessness. Any little dreams one might have had were and are destroyed in the hood; potential is lost and aspirations fade. The culprit is an unconscious way of thinking that is taught and learned, as young people become resilient within a hopeless mindset.

Hip-hop brings the hope back. Even if it offers no change, it at least gives confirmation that your situation is recognized and identified. The hip-hop culture being birthed out of this anxiety has created a new voice of resistance for a disenfranchised group of people. Young people needed a way to begin understanding the struggles of urban life, and the hip-hop subculture, using rap as its medium, was the vehicle that would speak into this culture and be its voice to the world.

Today, however, the questions "Where is hip-hop going? Where am I going?" are important as we see hip-hop moving away from addressing the serious struggles and issues faced by the people in urban communities. It has moved toward celebrating the materialistic, money- and sex-driven life of a "baller shot caller." This is a loss. Hip-hop is in danger of losing its core identity and greater purpose as it is watered down.

If you ask a student from the inner city, "Who is A. Philip Randolph?" "How about Marcus Garvey? Garrett Morgan?"—and in some cases even "Who is Dr. Martin Luther King?"—they may tell you, "Just somebody from black history." The adage "If you do not know where you came from, you will never know where you are going" fits here. If hip-hop shifts from voicing the struggle of everyday trying to make it, trying to find my way in this corrupt system, to voicing a pseudo-struggle of chasing dollars and fronting as if I have "made it" with my one CD that went platinum, then its authentic identity will break down or be lost altogether.

Now I am not saying that hip-hop is the only reason students fail to learn their history. That would be lame. Rather, our whole society is sick, valuing quick-fix hits. The problems are evident in our weak educational systems and self-seeking politicians' tendency to do what is best for themselves versus what's best for the people.

PHIL: WHAT MUSIC DOES

Music is powerful, and it has the power to move hearts, motivate moods and challenge thought, but this power is not unique to hip-hop. Music is the medium human beings reach for to give voice to and clarify their struggles. The medium of rap music brings clarity to the subculture of hip-hop and opens the door for the world to listen and seek to understand a subculture that is screaming to be heard. And it numbs our pain: "One thing 'bout music, when it hit, you feel no pain" (Dead Prez, "Hip-Hop," from *lets get free* LP).

Let's make the picture personal. You are riding in your car and the radio is playing something, but you're not really paying attention to it as you surf the stations. Then that one song hits, and all conversation stops. The volume button is turned up until the speakers crack and your head starts rocking; the rearview mirror, cell phone or whatever you have in your hand becomes a mic.

You start spitting (rapping) the lyrics from Jay-Z: "If you feeling like a pimp man . . . gone brush ya shoulders off . . . you betta get that dirt off ya shoulders." Suddenly your car has been transformed into a concert hall, and you are rapping on stage at "Hooptie Arena." Deep inside in some unexplainable way, you have been, if only for a moment, *revived.*

I cannot count how many times I was jamming so much that I pulled my car over because the music was just too good and everyone in the car had to sing or rhyme every verse at the top of their lungs. To focus on driving was irrelevant at the time; we just had to stop.

One day I had just bought the Run-DMC all-time classic hits collection, and as soon as I put the CD in, my friends Efrem Smith and Fred Lynch and I all started to rhyme as loud as we could. Every hook, every verse and every beat was met with a head bounce, and yes, the car was pulled over and doors opened as we finished one song after another. We walked around the car like we were Run-DMC, rhyming these cuts as if the album had been just released.

It was as if the songs took us somewhere that we had long since left behind and were now remembering. Life was fresh all over again; in this brief moment we could escape all our worries, because our lives are intertwined with the culture of hip-hop.

What is it in music that brings such a gut response? Certain songs, from rap, R&B, rock and country (well, maybe not country!) to gospel, penetrate through the darkness of our lives and turn us from thoughts of depression to hopefulness, from a sense of love lost to a love gained, to feel and even realize our potential and be motivated toward change.

One of the underlying reasons music does this is that it provides us with a feeling of being understood. The artist has been able to pinpoint something real in our life and speak about it with influence and power. Music is the number-one coping mechanism in the life of young people, while Mom is, say, forty-ninth on the list and Dad (if he is around) is fifty-fifth.

PHIL: HIP-HOP HISTORY LESSON

Here's how a current high school student put it all together:

"Back before Rakim became a microphone fiend
Kool Herc was in the Bronx rockin' the DJ scene.
Sugarhill Gang was number one on the charts
Grandmaster Flash and Melle Mel turned 'The Message'
    into art.
Rick Rubin and Russell Simmons started Def Jam
LL and EPMD were on the label back then.
Maybe you don't know, Juice Crew battled Boogie Down
    Productions
Cops began to run when they heard KRS-One.
Then the god Rakim and DJ Eric B. blew the game open
In the project buildings of Staten Island, Wu-Tang started
    formin'.
Nas was lookin' out his window for material
Suge Knight with his hand on rap's neck, had the game in a
    stranglehold.
Remember Kwame had the polka dots and crazy haircut?
Phife was tellin' y'all to get some toilet paper cuz ya lyrics
    is butt.
An MC named Christopher Wallace started rocking in
    Brooklyn

When Tupac Shakur was hangin' in Oakland.
Kris Kross hangin' with JD before Bow Wow,
Public Enemy encouraging a nation of millions to be proud.
Ice Cube was AmeriKKKa's Most Wanted
Before Gang Starr and Krumb Snatcha started makin' em pay.
Grandmaster Caz, Kurtis Blow, DJ Red Alert,
Battlin' Mr. Magic, the war between radio networks.
Of course we lost some soldiers: Poetic, Buffy, Cowboy,
    Scott La Rock
Big L, Big Pun, Eazy-E, Biggie Smalls and 2Pac.
Camouflage died, too, everybody in Savannah miss him
And a piece of Magnolia died with Souljah Slim.
The Hip-Hop history lesson, know ya facts
Cuz rap's more than just earning stacks."

("ONE LOVE," ADAM LEVIN)

I can remember listening to Whodini, Biggie, Poor Righteous Teachers, Afrika Bambaataa, Grandmaster Flash and the Furious Five, the Fat Boys, KRS-ONE, Run-DMC, Eric B. and Rakim, and Tupac, chilling in my room after some girl broke up with me, or just dealing with life growing up. This music, along with that of Earth, Wind and Fire, the Commodores, AWB and others, brought peace of mind and helped me understand life and put it in perspective.

So hip-hop takes rap—the primary medium to send and fund its message—to meet a need that people didn't know they had until verses were spit and a connection was made. Now a voice of a generation is being heard in order to empower an otherwise powerless class of people.

But then there can be a backlash. My friend Michael Eric Dyson says it this way: "It is difficult for a culture that is serious about the maintenance of social arrangements, economic conditions, and political choices that create and reproduce poverty, racism, sexism, classism, and violence to display a significant appreciation for musical expressions that contest the existence of such problems in black and Latino communities" (*Reflecting Black*, p. 7). When you break this quote down, Mike is saying that the dominant culture—either white majority or those influenced by dominant-culture mindset, no matter what the color—have established social arrangements that limit opportunities for the class of people who are creating hip-hop culture. Thus when artists rap about it, bang out a video articulating the struggle of their ghetto existence, yet make money on it so that they can escape that ghetto existence, the dominant culture becomes frustrated about these messages, because the system they established is now being used against them.

It is important to understand that *hip-hop exists to get on your nerves!* It gets on your nerves because it forces the listener to rethink their entire existence as it questions societal structures. Hip-hop exposes lies and provokes thought, leaving listeners grasping for something to hold on to as their assumptions about life are challenged. One example of what this looks like is the verses spit by the rap artist Jadakiss in the hot song "Why" of 2004: "Why they gotta open your package and read your mail / Why they stop lettin' niggaz get degreez in jail . . . / Why Halle have to let a white man pop her to get a Oscar / Why Denzel have to be crooked before he took it."

Such questions could make you feel uncomfortable, if you come from the dominant-culture mindset, or they could connect with you as deeply as if you were listening to a song in church. Being connected means that you count, and when a young person counts they know that they belong. Hip-hop does that—it creates within itself a vibe where people can count and thus belong.

This is why hip-hop has been postmodern from its inception, seeming rebellious to the mainstream but a breath of fresh air to the everyday folk, audaciously confronting the system with questions that no one has been bold enough to ask. An example of postmodern intentional defiance can be found in the truth commercials (see www.thetruth.com) about cigarettes and how tobacco companies seek to manipulate the consumer. They don't rap, they don't do anything that you would see at a hip-hop concert, but when you see them you could say, "That's hip-hop." Hip-hop has given urban culture a voice where otherwise it would have been kept silent.

Unlike its parents (blues, jazz and the like), hip-hop has manifested itself in several different ways; therefore its impact is broader. In hip-hop history, when parties were thrown and the deejays were spinning while the emcees rapped, the police would come and arrest everyone at the party for disturbing the peace. Because the music was new, strange, loud and not as understandable as R&B and other types of music of the day, it was a threat. Therefore parents of kids at the party would call and ask for it to be shut down.

So hip-hop was created amid great tension, and in the minds of some still today, hip-hop carries connotations of illegality and should be banned. Only in 1979, when the SugarHill Gang came out with "Rapper's Delight," which sold two million and stayed on the *Billboard* chart for twelve weeks reaching up to number thirty-six, did hip-hop stop being seen as illegal.

HIP-HOP CULTURE CARRIERS

There are at least ten expressions of hip-hop that are readily recognizable to everyone in the culture of hip-hop. Hip-hoppers may not all be able to explain all of these expressions, but they understand them intuitively and acknowledge them as hip-hop:

- deejayin'
- emceeing

- breaking
- graffiti art
- street language
- street entrepreneurship
- beat box
- street knowledge
- street fashion
- hip-hop spirituality

Deejayin'/Turntableist. This person mixes records and often uses the record itself as the instrument by scratching it against the needle. The deejay was the first to come on the scene, bringing all their records and sound systems to a park or a house party and starting to mix the records together. Kool Herc was the pioneer of all the deejays of New York, and for that matter all of hip-hop. Originally from Kingston, Jamaica, he moved to New York in 1968 and brought with him his deejayin' skills. Deejays in Jamaica had developed a unique style, talking over the instrumental records; this was called toasting. Kool Herc would ride down streets in the Bronx with huge speakers sticking up from the backseat of his convertible.

Another deejay from the South Bronx, Grandmaster Flash, began to get into the technology of the art. In 1977—still before any commercial rap record was out—Flash created a style of dropping short, fast beats from all types of records while maintaining a perpetual groove so that dancers never missed a step. After a while Melle Mel and the Furious Five became Grandmaster Flash's rap group. Around the same time, also in the South Bronx, a deejay named Theodore invented a technique known now as scratching. While one record was spinning and people were dancing, a record being played on another turntable was used as an instrument to create effects that complemented the beat.

A deejay such as Grandmaster Flash would come out to a park and spin, and that's how a party started. An emcee would come along and spit on the mic but would give props back to his deejay, and the crowd would flow with the emcee and the deejay in concert with each other.

Emceeing/Rapping. This artist gets on the microphone and chants verses that rhyme or phrases that don't rhyme but that rhythmically flow with the music. These lyrics tell a story, teach morals or history, give a report on street life, or celebrate life. The quality of lyrics eventually came to be dictated by record labels, unfortunately, in order to move CDs off the shelf rather than move people for change.

Breaking. B-boys and B-girls put together spectacular combinations of moves with gymnastics, capoeira (a style of martial arts originating from Africans who were enslaved by Brazilians) and couples spinning (called windmills), synchronized with the break beats of the songs the deejay spins. As Kool Herc's reputation grew, breakers would follow him at all his parties, and from there breaking took off all over New York.

Breakers started out in New York dance clubs. Members of rival gangs would be thrown out if they fought, so they "battled" using dance. To these cats, dance was not a lifestyle, just something to do to pass the time. African Americans made up the first groups of breakers, but as that began to fade, groups of Puerto Rican teens picked it up. Breaking involves a style of communication all its own. Dancers use various mixes of dance moves in order to create movement in sync with the break beat of the record.

Graffiti artists/Bombers/Tag artists. Also called taggers, burners or bombers, these are the street artists who spray paint on trains, walls or abandoned buildings. Because graffiti was illegal, as hip-hop was when it started out, it was all the more exciting. All the crews went by tag (code) names; hence the term *tagging*. Hip-hop promoters back in the day would have graffiti artists design their flyers and other promotional items.

Street language. Hip-hop has its own vocabulary; it is as changing as the wind, but at the same time it has a certain stability necessary to make sense of life. It is coded language that informs the culture through metaphors and abstract images to express what is experienced. A created language is a sign of creative intelligence. Missionaries seek to communicate to a tribe or other people group who have never had their language written down, working with them to form letters or shapes for their alphabet. So it is in hip-hop; however, many words as commonly used in the English language do not carry the meaning that the hip-hop culture seeks to communicate. Often a word's meaning is totally different in the hip-hop culture from what it is in mainstream culture.

For example, consider the phrase "Thug Life," which was coined by Tupac and generated a whole movement. The typical person outside of hip-hop culture who sees "Thug Life" tattooed on someone's arm, shoulder or stomach (as was the case with Pac) will turn away and maybe feel disrespected, thinking, *How can anyone promote such hate!* Yet the code in this phrase means more than what is evident on the surface. The phrase is actually an acronym for "The Hate U Gave Little Infants F- - - - Everybody!" Now, this is raw, but it points to a biblical truth. Think of Galatians 5:7: "God cannot be mocked. A man reaps what he sows." "Thug Life" is saying that life for some is terribly harsh and unjust. The life of kids in the hood can and has produced men who are angry for life. Over time, a corrupt system, poor education and economic troubles can cause bitterness and frustration toward everybody.

Street entrepreneurship. "Making something out of nothing"—that is the task of the street entrepreneur, or "trying to make a dollar out of fifteen cents." The hustle man mindset marks someone who has to figure out each day what can put food on the table, and until that question is answered the intensity of the need continues to increase. This does not mean just selling drugs on the corner, even though that means of getting cash is one facet of street entrepreneurship.

Beat box. Creating a beat with whatever you had was essential, and thus the beat box was invented by using what you had, your mouth. The original beat box makers were Doug E. Fresh, the Fat Boyz and Biz Markie. If you weren't looking, you wouldn't realize it was a human being making that noise; you would have thought it was a record.

Street knowledge. The knowledge of the streets is about survival—dealing with all the realities of life and knowing how to "get over on the system" with this knowledge. Common says, "There is a difference from being raised in the hood and just living in the hood." If you move to the city because of the lofts and better commute, you will not have a street understanding when it comes to survival. But if you were raised in the hood, whether or not you got involved with the business of the hood, you grew up with a different mindset and a different set of eyes: you look at things through the lens of hood politics.

Street fashion. When Run-DMC said, "Don't want nobody's name on my behind," the message was clear: we want our own fashion, and it better be tight. With the rise and fall of fads as well the stiff competition between apparel lines, nobody could give hip-hop an image except hip-hop itself. The look of hip-hop is not really describable except when you see it. Run-DMC provided the first consistent image of hip-hop as they rocked with the black jeans, black shirt, black hat and white Adidases with no shoestrings.

Run-DMC's promotion of Adidas on their album caused the shoe company to take notice. Once at a concert in Madison Square Garden, Run told the crowd to put their Adidases in the air, and countless people held up their Adidases with no shoe-strings. After Run-DMC got off stage, an Adidas rep was right there with an endorsement deal.

Now companies such as Phat Farm, Sean John and South Pole are connected to the culture and are able to provide the look that is distinctive. In New York, Dapper Dan's shop was where you went to get your gear and then get it stitched up to whatever look you wanted on your jacket, jeans or shirt, so you could rock in your Gucci or Louis Vuitton with your fashion signature on it.

Spirituality. After Afrika Bambaataa (which means "affection-ate leader") cut his ties from the Black Spades, one of the largest gangs in the Bronx, he started the Zulu Nation (named for a tribe in southern Africa), seeking to bring peace to the hood through hip-hop music and dance. Bambaataa saw a spiritual connection between the music of hip-hop and the lifestyle that it birthed. He adopted principles of the Zulu people, which included unity, love, happiness, fun and discipline, and created a positive connection with people who were seeking refuge from the streets. Though these principles aren't explicitly Christian, that does not mean they don't have value in terms of being able to affect people's lives positively. We as Christians have to look for ways to connect with others and bring the light of the gospel to them.

Hip-hop has always had a spiritual base simply because it is tied to music. All music has a spiritual mood to it, so when you bring thought into it to provoke change, it becomes spiritual. (Of course I am referring to a general understanding of spirituality, not one defined by any particular religion.) There are elements where one is able to sustain some mode of sanity while seeking to ex-press yourself through hip-hop. Artist such as Poor Righteous Teachers, KRS-ONE, De la Soul, the Fugues, Arrested Develop-ment, Mos Def, Talib Kwali, Tribe Called Quest and others have sought to foment a sense of spirituality in their hip-hop lyrics. The god of hip-hop has no real standard and is not offended when be-havior and belief don't match up. This is even more of a reason for followers of Christ to bring a clear, relevant, biblically sensitive message to the hip-hop culture.

RAP'S DIVORCE FROM HIP-HOP

Now each of these foundational culture carriers making up hip-hop culture is unique; however, it is rap that stands out above them all in the minds of most people. Rap was and still is the most market-able of all the elements (at least economically). With the help of record companies, however, rap moved in a natural progression to divorce itself from hip-hop's other elements in the mid 1980s. Pro-ducers and promoters saw that rap artists were the only ones cre-ating a conversation with the crowd and that people demanded more from the artist; here they recognized an opportunity.

It was easier to bring one or two rappers with a deejay or tracks than to contract a deejay and all his or her equipment along with breakers and their crews and taggers. What became obvious was that the economic gain from this new musical genre and culture would come from rap; whoever had the gift to move the crowd (emceeing) was also going to be moving dollars into his or her pockets. The other elements just would not hold a crowd or sell LPs.

UNDOING FALSE LINKS

Remember that hip-hop is more than the art of rap; it began to meet certain core needs of a generation before the generation could articulate the needs they had. Some needs in the lives of the urban African American community, in fact, are being met only by hip-hop.

However, this has not been recognized by many in the Euro-American evangelical community. Thus very few in that community honestly seek to reach this culture or see any redeeming value in hip-hop, let alone any way to use it for the kingdom. This is the tension about Christendom and hip-hop: most Euro-American evangelicals are so separate from "the world" that they don't really know what issues urban people are facing.

Hip-hop, in fact, calls attention to the failures of government, schools, police, preachers and churches, bringing them to light while shaming them at the same time.

Now I am not saying that all rap artists and their music are all righteous. There are serious contradictions within hip-hop and in their messages, lifestyles and overall representations of the culture. These artists need to be held accountable in some way regarding the content of their raps and its impact in the lives of the most impressionable students they influence.

Still, when people from the dominant culture or a dominant-culture mindset are dissing rap music and hip-hop culture as if they had no redeeming value, in essence they're saying that those who hip-hop's messages are coming from, and those they are being sent to, have no redeeming value either.

You yourself may see hip-hop as an unredeemable hindrance to the kingdom. I ask you to open your mind to the truth that God created all things to give him glory but that people who are separated from God take these good things and just mess them up. However, when these things are touched again by God, the content changes; the vessel may remain the same, but its content has changed. Isaiah acknowledged that he was "a man of unclean lips" and came from "a people of unclean lips," but when God touched his mouth he was cleansed. And when God asked, "Who will go for us?" he said, "Send me!" (see Isaiah 6:5-8). Similarly, I come from the hip-hop culture, a people of unclean lips, and I am unclean. But once I have been touched by God, do I have to become part of mainstream church culture in order to be a follower of Christ?

There is a chainlink fence that we must cut down if we are to understand hip-hop and begin real conversations that can lead to making an impact on this generation for the cause of Jesus Christ. Let's look at links that must be cut from this fence before hip-hop and Christians can understand each other and together answer the question, why is the subculture of hip-hop so significant for the postmodern generation? Once the answer is understood and applied, we can begin to work toward transforming this culture for the kingdom of God.

THE IDENTITY LINK

Cutting the first link involves acknowledging that hip-hop's sustainability does not rely on the medium of its message, rap, but on the identity it provides to a people group that have never really had an identity of their own. Ask yourself this question: What people group in America has had their identity taken from them and their dignity denied, has been exploited the most for others' profit, and has had their life shaped by strife and injustice?

When you examine groups of U.S. immigrants and their exodus from their homeland, you will find that some did not have a choice in leaving to try to make a better life for themselves, while those who did have a choice were for the most part able to move with all their culture, dignity and identity intact. Consider the differences among the cases of African slaves, Haitians and Cubans. And if you went to the west side of Chicago and took a walk from South Lawndale to North Lawndale, you would see a big difference between the two cultures of these communities.

In Little Village (South Lawndale), which is mostly Latino—first- and second-generation Mexican—the shops and restaurants reveal not just an Americanized Mexican community with Spanish hip-hop blasting. Rather, store owners play music from their homeland, and the food, language and customs of that community reflect a deep appreciation of who they are and their culture of origin. It is a bustling community; in fact, within the Chicago metro area the cash flow along Twenty-Sixth Street is second only to the Magnificent Mile shopping district in downtown Chicago. Little Village's banks, bridal shops and grocery stores are distinctive to that community and are owned by its members.

But when you walk one block over to North Lawndale, populated mostly by African Americans, and start looking for anything that reflects an African culture, identity or cultural way of life, you will not find it. We African Americans have never really expressed our own distinctly African identity in America independent of slavery. Nor has the African culture been valued by us, let alone esteemed by the broader dominant society. Various forms of African American identity shapers (Kwanzaa, African rites of passage, etc.) have been advocated as means to bring value and self-awareness, but they came late and have not been widely appreciated and appropriated because of other psychosocial issues.

Hip-hop came along as a way to bring meaning at a time when young African Americans needed a voice to proclaim what life is for them. When students know they count, they know that they belong. This need is universal, but it is heightened in the lives of youth living in impoverished situations. For years the African American community sought to fit in, to count, but never did. When belonging is a prevailing need, you will find a place or even create a place where you belong. Thus hip-hop culture.

THE PROPHET LINK

To understand real hip-hop, it's important to understand and grasp the difference between rappers and emcees. There are thousands of rappers but only a few emcees. A rapper is for the industry or produced by the industry; they rap about whatever is popular, and they give the culture of hip-hop a reputation of only being about materialism and sex. (If you saw the rapping Dalma-tians in the movie *Brown Sugar,* you'll understand the difference.) An emcee, on the other hand, seeks to keep the purity in hip-hop and stays away from the entertainment, performance-only view that rappers consistently have. The emcee is considered to be a lyricist with something to say that's for your heart, your soul or your intellect. They don't rhyme about what is popular or impor-tant to the materialistic hip-hop head because they are stewards of the culture and hip-hop's message. Emcees are seeking to drop some knowledge about life and how best to live in this world. These artists get drowned out by others who are staining the foundation of hip-hop. We need to listen closely to artists such as Mos Def, Common, Talib Kweli, Biggie, Run-DMC, Poor Right-eous Teachers and Arrested Development, who are seeking to keep "hip-pocrisy" out of hip-hop. The message they bring would not be called a Christian message, but it still deals with issues that affect all humanity. These artists are the true skilled lyricists who are serious about their art.

Hip-hop helps us to appreciate the culture of people who have overcome obstacles and now, instead of setting up obstacles against you, seek to empower you to move with juice. Consider Thomas Dorsey, who used his God-given gift in music in the clubs playing the blues. Yet as his conviction was to play music for the church, he took the sounds that he knew and created what we know today as gospel music.

THE NEEDS LINK

We cut the next link when we acknowledge that the needs that hip-hop meets are powerful. These needs have become more ev-ident as hip-hop has grown into a culture and had an impact on all of society. They are met through the artists and their music, though record labels and through us, the broader community that constantly seeks out this music and culture. Hip-hop is scratching an itch that no other musical genre was able to scratch at the time. I'm going to break these needs down in a three-part process. First we look at the need that exists in culture; second how this need is met; third the outcome of what we may see as this itch is scratched.

The need to be heard. The urban community is an oral communication culture—information is transmitted quickly and verbally. The need to get my point across, speak my mind or just teach has always been dominated by the oral communication culture. The campaign to "Just say no" to drugs was noble but the reason it failed in urban communities was because it was too literate. People are not illiterate, but this kind of attack on a social norm needed to be quick and oral. In order to impact this culture with the gospel of Jesus Christ your communication must be verbal as well as expressive. It is not only what you say but also how it's said.

Conflict-interactive communication. A conscious emcee would bring all the points of the argument up before giving you their final opinion. It is an interactive debate with the intention to persuade you one way or the other. In the city, communication and confrontation coexist. People are arguing or they may be simply communicating. The other key to how this is expressed is that the sender of the message is also the receiver of the same message. Hip-hop is sender-receiver friendly, in that the person rapping will not say something that they themselves do not understand or are not in agreement with from their background. Now as we extract this process to seek to reach this culture with the gospel, the church must be sender-receiver friendly. Most churches are only sender friendly and hope the young people or whomever will just understand.

The three R's. You know you have been hit with hip-hop communication structure when it is *real, relevant* and *respectful.* The first R is *real.* Real is all that hip-hop culture is based on. So much of what we see is false and covered up by media that when the truth is leaked it is almost unbelievable because of the lies that we have been dwelling in. Therefore, when you hear an emcee rap about pimping, shooting, hustling, racism and life on the street for a single parent, you as the receiver of this communication feel like someone now understands your plight, rather than just ignoring it like everyone else. The next R is *relevant.* You know when you have communicated to the culture when you are on top of what is going on now and sometimes how current issues relate to the past. Hip-hop is always changing yet remaining the same all at once. The last key value of hip-hop is being *respectful.* The unity in hip-hop is what makes it so multicultural. The cat everyone perceives as a nerd is welcomed in the hip-hop world as an equal. Hip-hop puts aside judgment about everything from lifestyle to religious views and invites everyone in.

The need to transfer values. Often the messages of hip-hop speak into the lives of those in the culture concerning what is important to them. Hip-hop passes on cultural values that will shape a generation, as well as bring about a new style of acceptable behavior. The need to learn how to make it in this cold world exists. KRS-ONE called himself the "Teacher" because he was the first emcee to start teaching black history through rap. He called his style of rhyming "edutainment." By getting the best of education and of entertainment, he was able to pass on insights that his listeners had never heard; and now they might pick up a book to dig a little deeper—which might help them in their desire to do better than the generation before.

Shaping an identity of self and spiritual formation. Throughout hip-hop culture there is a need to find oneself. The messages in the music, though not overtly Christian, contain spiritual principles and ethical realities that cannot be denied. Thus, the average hip-hop head listening to DMX, a rapper whose name means Dark Man X and who has a prayer at the beginning of each of his CDs, is now influenced by the mixed message he gets from DMX. Yet the listener might also be turned on to the thought that maybe, just maybe, God will hear my prayer. Because there isn't a clear message concerning who God is, what God expects and how to live for God, hip-hop brings a mix of religion and spirituality that is more accessible to your average searching person.

Lyrical content. Artists such as Slick Rick, Grandmaster Flash, Poor Righteous Teachers, De La Soul, Common and others seek to teach through their lyrics. This is done at the expense of record sales, fame and popularity because they aren't rapping about pimps, pushers and hoes. Over the last decade, the artists who wouldn't have risked rapping about social issues for fear of losing their audience are now stepping up. New artists are rapping about the issues they face and are stimulating their audience to think more critically about what they hear and see around them. The artists who are hitting the wave of critically thinking hip-hop heads are becoming more well known, and their style is like a breath of fresh air to the manure that is on the air waves now. A new generation of shows are popping up to reach this people group (Def Poetry) who are and have grown up on hip-hop and poetry, and thus are not wanting to buy into the candy lyrics that other emcees are rhyming about.

The need for authenticity. Tupac said he was always looking for "real n-----." He was looking for the brothas or sistas who could hold life down and succeed against all odds. The need to find authentic people is a cry all of us share, no matter what and where you have been in your life; it is in consistent sincerity that brings authenticity.

There are so many people in the rap game that are just wanting to use it as a get-rich scheme and hold the culture hostage with their rendition of what is real, but in actuality, it is not. People making ends meet on the street every day are looking for the people who have their back and will not fake them out when things get rough.

The church is not seen as authentic because it has lost its edge to be committed to the widows and orphans (the modern-day single mother and the children without fathers or any parent raising them). Therefore, when the street sees the church they see people who are commuting from the world to the church but never blending the two together. Thus, the impact is then seen as self-seeking rather than as sincere and authentic.

Framework of African American-male posturing. Respect for African American males has hit an all-time low, yet at the same time, it is African American males who are influencing the hip-hop market. The fact that hip-hop is a male-dominated industry is obvious, thus the need to be even more authentic. Who else could represent authenticity besides the most endangered, most feared, most despised and most hated of humans: the Black Male. Here you have an entire industry filled with successful African American men who have struggled to make the American dream of money, power and sex come true through hip-hop music, but now, in spite of their success, they are not looked upon any more favorably.

In the process of meeting the need to be authentic, a framework of spirituality and of manhood is developed to provide a blueprint for one's identity as a man. Often the images of what this man looks like are not positive.

Shared knowledge. Authenticity is lived out in hip-hop through three different scenarios. First, it is proven over the long haul. The emcees who have and are still able to bring the real on the mic and have not tripped over their own pride are those who get mad love from the culture. The founders of hip-hop—KRS-ONE, Run-DMC and Jam Master J, Grandmaster Flash, Kool Herc, Kurtis

Blow and others—are always referenced by the younger emcees because they have been real and around for the long haul.

Second is the validity of the emcee and how strong they can give street life a message. The street prophet is almost like a prophet from the Old Testament in which they would be killed if their prophecy didn't come true. The same thing happens to the emcee whose street prophecies are not authentic: their career is dead.

Third is the need for African American masculinity to be validated through the positive skills they have in order to use them to improve their lives and others.

The need to be socially interactive. Emcees and record labels, like other artists, use their positions to push their social and political interest. There is a need to create an irritation that will force those in authority to hear those who are left out of the mainstream decision-making process yet who have to live with the consequences. The need to be socially active stems from the real gospel of hip-hop, which is justice.

Bringing awareness to the issues. Coded language is one process used in hip-hop to be socially interactive. The need to speak in such a way that it doesn't give too much information but just enough to rally hearers. Record labels bring their artists to voter registration drives to push for their candidates. The voter drive during the last presidential election put forth by P-Diddy was very successful, as it pertained to the minority voters registered. Although the election didn't go the way P-Diddy wanted, it showed the strength of the hip-hop community when they needed to unify their people on the issues.

Battles. Battling was a style of male and female posturing and confronting without physical fighting (most of the time). Two different emcees would go head to head against each other, each with a time limit, and they would have to rhyme off the top of their head punch line after punch line about their opponent. These emcee battles in rap's early days brought about an example of what justice could look like based on a topic, skill and subject. For example, EPMD held several battles over a song called "Roxanne." In these call and response rhymes, the girl told her issue of what she would do for her man and what she wouldn't do for her man, while the man told what he would or wouldn't do for his girl. Other emcees created different battle raps, which became more serious than a girlfriend or boyfriend thing. These groups created a voice to speak about their issues when no one else would, and their social commentary about life brought about certain movements.

In the 80s, rappers dropped their beefs with each other and came together for a single called "Self-Destruction." This was a social commentary about violence in the city, gun violence specifically, and from this they created several pockets of impact toward stopping the violence.

Now, as the church seeks to connect with or understand hiphop, culture issues of justice (such as police brutality, racism and overwhelming poverty) must not be overlooked. When the church ignores these issues then the church's message to this culture becomes watered down and ignored.

THE DIVERSITY LINK

Cutting the final link off this fence to allow a bridge of better understanding involves recognizing hip-hop's strength to stimulate and attract diversity. Sprite did a five-year survey and found that if they could sell a given product to the African American male, then they could sell it to anybody. Hip-hop attracts a holistic diversity, as it infuses all socioeconomic groups and puts them on equal ground. Cornel West states its impact:

The Afro-Americanization of white youth has been more a

male than female affair given the prominence of male athletes and the cultural weight of male pop artist. This process results in white youth—male and female—imitating and emulating black male styles of walking, talking, dressing. Though imprisoned in record numbers, their styles have become disproportionately influential in popular culture.

(RACE MATTERS)

The way hip-hop brings together people from all walks of life should embarrass the church, the body of Christ, given that the most segregated hour in America is still Sunday morning. Hip-hop's path into diversity was not planned; it just happened. The music and the message hit nerves in all kinds of people. Two factors probably explain why this happened. First, hip-hop, and its message, is real. People can relate to you if you are real. Second was the time in which hip-hop was birthed. The kids whose parents were of the 1960s and 1970s and had seen little or no change were now ready to live out the dream of diversity. Without "trying to be diverse," they just lived it.

The church needs to learn a lesson here. To move with intentionality toward diversity, we will have to apply the words that have been sung in churches all over: "Come just as you are"! The language we use in the church and our long delay in living out our message are what weakens our testimony to the world, especially to the hip-hop culture. We need to gain sensitivity and move toward understanding hip-hop culture without judgment. In so doing we will begin speaking to this culture about the gospel it is in desperate need of.

3

BLUES AND NEGRO SPIRITUALS, THE PARENTS OF Hip-Hop

The blues functioned for another generation of blacks much as rap functions for young blacks today: as a source of racial identity permitting forms of boasting and asserting machismo for devalued black men suffering from social degradation, allowing commentary on social and personal conditions in uncensored language, and fostering the ability to transform hurt and anguish into art and commerce.

(MICHAEL ERIC DYSON, *REFLECTING BLACK*)

When you don't know the struggle of a people, you don't know the people. Black and Latino theologians, pastors, youth ministers and poets have to speak of theology out of their social context, the struggle of poverty and disenfranchisement. In the African American experience, struggle is a way of life and is best expressed through the arts and especially music. Music is and always will be the most complete tool for expressing the pains of any disenfranchised group, to help them make sense out of life and building some sense of sanity.

As we listen to the blues, Negro spirituals and hip-hop, we feel our existence more powerfully. A recognition of what I'm going through infused with the blues, Negro spirituals or hip-hop creates a refreshing peace, a sense that someone understands, and stimulates hope within an otherwise (from the world's perspective) hopeless situation.

When I was growing up, my mom, who is white and has been serving as a social worker in the hood for over thirty years, said to me once that white people don't have to ask themselves what it means to be white whenever they go anywhere. This statement meant a lot to me growing up in a multiethnic household. I took that statement and sought to develop that type of confidence, coming at life from a stronger point of view than my peers and seeing myself as a coequal of those from the dominant culture. (When I speak of the dominant culture, I mean any group of people who are insensitive to the needs of others and lack the desire to understand those needs, all the while increasing the gap through classism and economic and racial conflicts.)

The dominant culture—from the perspective of the minority culture—looks at life from a self-centered vantage point, a me-for-me mindset. This is oppressive to those who are not a part of the mainstream culture. I remember reading in college about how the dominant culture communicates versus how the minority culture communicates. In the dominant culture's style of communication, statements are made in conversation and simply left there for others to deal with. Without caring whether the listener has understood what they said, speakers from the dominant culture just move on to another point. The minority communication style, on the other hand, involves making sure that in regular conversations others understand what the subject is before the speaker moves on to another point. This is just one example of the unconscious dynamics that are obstacles to communication between a community that sees life through the lens of struggle and another community that doesn't.

The music of the blues and Negro spirituals reflects issues that were rarely covered on the evening news—the struggles and tensions of life for African Americans in both the North and the South. The blues and Negro spirituals explored the terrible tensions while creating hope in the midst of it all.

Growing up in the hood, you knew that you didn't have everything you wanted, but you had everything you needed. You didn't say you were poor; you really didn't know how poor you were until someone rocked some brand new Adidases. That was when it hit you: "Dang, we broke like mug." But one thing was for sure: whatever you were, everyone around you was it too. What music did, especially the blues, was to speak into your existence and help you make sense of what you were going through and what you felt while going through it. The blues put in word and rhythms the history of both the individual and the corporate struggle.

Storytelling was and still is the most important component in common among these musical genres. Storytelling is the key to transferring values, morals and ways of handling life struggles from one generation to the next. For example, the blues song called "I Don't Wanna Go to Vietnam" by Johnny Lee Hooker told stories about the people he misses who are fighting in the war and about a war at home in the United States. This song could be likened to Eminem's song "Toy Soldiers," dealing with President George W. Bush and expressing his concerns about the Iraq War. You could spend all day comparing and contrasting particular blues songs and their similarities with hip-hop lyrics. They all have one underlying theme, though: the struggles people in the hood are facing.

To the average parishioner accustomed to the traditional African American worship experience, comparing Negro spirituals to the blues, let alone hip-hop, may seem inappropriate, even sacrilegious. However, my intent is to compare the underlying themes that unify the messages of the three genres, not to validate various hip-hop messages that are contradictory to the message of spirituals.

There are three key similarities among these three musical expressions that we will get into: a connection to liberation, a need to transfer values, and coded language.

NEGRO SPIRITUALS AND HIP-HOP

The very first Negro spirituals were influenced by African music by way of the call-and-response style called "shouts," mixing dancing, clapping and foot tapping. This is the same thing the emcee does with the crowd, getting them to repeat the rapper's chants or hooks. This is not original with hip-hop; it comes from and out of African worship experiences.

Early spirituals were sung at camp meetings without hymnbooks, moving with a spontaneous rhythm. Often songs would be composed on the spot, drawing on skills very similar to those used in hip-hop's freestyle. In hip-hop freestyle, an emcee "battles" another emcee without any prerehearsed verses; off the top of their head, each is to compose rhymes that make sense and diss the other emcee. Freestyle panache requires a certain genius, a quick wit that can pile up rhyming phrases in a matter of seconds.

The Negro spirituals used coded language to alert slaves who were going to run away with indications of what time, where and even how they would be escaping. Some of the words had a dual meaning. Home, for example, could mean a home in heaven with God, or depending on who sang about it and when, it might speak of a place where slaves could live free. Negro spirituals such as "Swing Low, Sweet Chariot" and "The Gospel Train" were means of communicating to slaves who needed to know what was going to happen that night as well as to provide hope for all that God was near. Slaves who heard "Go Down Moses," then, would know that tonight freedom was coming by way of Harriet Tubman and her Freedom Train: "When Israel was in Egypt's land / Let my people go / Oppressed so hard they could not stand / Let my people go."

Coded language in hip-hop is used to explore life without outsiders being able to understand or exploit the message. In his *Ruminations*, KRS-ONE states that *chill* was the first redefined word that hip-hop gave America. Then other words and phrases came, such as *fresh, dope, funky fresh, three times dope* and others. Hip-hop's use of coded language is prompted by the same need that underlay coded language in Negro spirituals: the need to camouflage. Thus, hip-hop has its own language that is distinctive to the culture it is speaking to, and it keeps the dominant community out while seeking to advance hip-hop culture.

Thomas Dorsey, considered the father of black gospel music, composed several gospel songs that now would be considered sacred songs in the African American worship experience but were demonized by the church at first. Dorsey had the nerve to see and understand the times—a generation that needed a message through music that would cause them to turn back to the church. He brought in the blues guitar, the drum and other instruments from the club scene of the day. His gospel songs include "Precious Lord," written after the loss of his wife and child while she was giving birth, and his powerful "Peace in the Valley," which he wrote for Mahalia Jackson in 1937.

Soon, though, Dorsey got so discouraged because the church was demonizing his music and not hearing the voice of the next generation that he stopped playing for churches and went back to playing for clubs. Years later he received all types of awards and even was elected to the Georgia Music Hall of Fame, as others recognized his efforts and even the church slowly warmed up to his style.

Thomas A. Dorsey's struggles highlight the church's hypocrisy—the same hypocrisy that makes many in the hip-hop community feel that the church is not for them. Often certain cultural expressions or practices are demonized by the church, or ignored; only much later, either by pressure or by force, the church begins to welcome the very thing it had criticized. Andrae Crouch sang "Oh Happy Day," and the church jumped on him and complained that his message was not spiritual enough; then after a while you find churches singing these songs as if they wrote them.

After Dorsey and Andrae Crouch, the hypocritical reactions continued against the Winans, who were ripped because they didn't say enough Jesus in their music. Then, moving into the twenty-first century, you find Kirk Franklin getting hit with a new type of shot from the church that has not acknowledged its own double-talk. That is, while the African American congregation was tripping over trivia with the music, the preachers were having sex with the church secretary and spending the offering on their car payments—but when it came to music, they were all self-righteousness.

Today hip-hop, which did not start in the church, is the target of church attacks based on its lack of reverence for tradition. But just as W. E. B. DuBois called African American spirituals "the slave's one articulate message to the world," hip-hop is a message to the world about the complexities of life for youth and young adults who are outside of the system. Like the Negro spirituals, hip-hop is concerned with liberation from bondage.

THE BLUES AND HIP-HOP

Bobby "Blue" Bland says it like this in his historic jam "Stormy Monday Blues": "They call it stormy Monday but Tuesday's just as bad (repeat 2), / Wednesday's worst and Lord and Thursday's oh so sad. / The eagle flies on Friday and Saturday I go out to play (repeat 2), / Sunday I go to church, and I kneel down and pray!"

The blues, like Negro spirituals, were built upon the telling of stories in which values, morals and history are expressed in song format, to teach and transform thinking without the listener's even knowing. Both were birthed out of situations of struggle and tension. The blues delved into human experiences that include negative outcomes. This music was real, raw and grassroots; it didn't sugarcoat anyone's issues, needs and desires. The blues addressed issues and struggles the church was not ready to deal with, and for this reason it was labeled "the devil's music." For those not really caring about church to the degree that it was their life, the blues functioned for them as the Negro spirituals did for those in the church. It was as if the blues spoke to the issues that the church wouldn't touch. Rap, too, often leads the listener to think, *Hey, this is what life is really like,* as it takes up issues that the church has been unwilling to talk about—and deals with them in ways that are disliked by the dominant culture.

The blues are considered to have started in 1912, with "The Memphis Blues" by W. C. Handy. The word *blues* in some respects means something quite different from what people usually think—that the blues are about the discouraged times of life, the time when my dog left with my wife, the pain of this or that. *Blues* is actually about getting your feelings off your chest. When blues artists are singing and using an instrument such as the harmonica, guitar or piano, they are bringing relief for themselves and their audience.

The blues came out of an array of backgrounds, but the sound that took over the world mostly grew out of the pain of life in the American South. Artists sang about everything, from Willie King and the Liberators' "Terrorized," about white America's terrorizing of African Americans, to Elmore James's "Talk to Me Baby (I Can't Hold On)," about his women and the pain of relationships between men and women.

As the blues were assimilated into mainstream America in the 1960s, they made a slow progression away from their roots and their people. Middle-class white kids began to gravitate to this culture and its music, while the African American generation that grew up on Muddy Waters, Bobby "Blue" Bland, Buddy Guy, Jimmy Rogers, Johnny Lee Hooker and Howling Wolf with their blues guitar sound started to fade, partly because they did not like attending events with middle-class white kids and partly because information about places and times of events didn't get to them. Before, word of mouth in the community would allow them to be aware of when and where a blues musician was playing, but now the white rock stations that broadcast the music and advertised events didn't make a marketing shift to reach the African American audience.

Here an interesting contrast comes up between blues and hip-hop. From its first commercial (LP) rap cut, "Rapper's Delight" by the SugarHill Gang, hip-hop has been bought and sold to 70 percent more whites than blacks, yet these ethnic groups have been able to assimilate into each other through hip-hop without watering down hip-hop's style and message.

Like hip-hop, blues has a message that can sound depressing and discouraging and can make you mad. Yet it is actually a release of what has been done or is being done. The pressure of this world makes me want to shout, and rap and the blues both allow me to do this shouting. Both also feature coded language, based in part on the artist's geographic location. Coded language is used in order for those inside the culture to hear certain buzz words that let them know I understand. The code hits those outside of the culture too, but it can be confusing and come across as antiestablishment (and it may be both of those things). One example of the code is found in the words "Thug Life," mentioned earlier, which mean "The Hate U Gave Little Infants F---- Everybody." The need is to create a language that gives a message to those who need to hear it.

Negro spirituals, the blues and hip-hop, then, have similar styles of message delivery and content. The need for the blues to speak about life's joys and pains in one generation caused hip-hop to arise to bring its message to its culture. Negro spirituals feature a basic liberation theology that has significant echoes in hip-hop.

Hip-Hop AS POSTMODERN CULTURE

Over the past couple of years I've been trying to gain a greater understanding of a conversation going on about postmodernity and the church. I've attended seminars, listened to panel discussions, and read books around the various issues surrounding postmodern culture and the church. Most of these discussions have been led by my brothers and sisters in a mostly suburban, white context. This has led me to wonder about an *urban* take on postmodernity. Is the discussion within the body of Christ about postmodern culture simply a context for understanding the culture of European Americans and suburbia? Or should all of those concerned about outreach, evangelism, and the relevance of the church regardless of race, location and denomination be in on the discussion?

If the discussions of postmodernity are to truly speak to urban culture and the emerging urban church, postmodernism must be looked at in the context of hip-hop culture and the African American journey. Putting the postmodern discussion in this light won't speak to the totality of urban culture, but it can at least begin sharpening our focus on emerging urban culture and the type of church needed to reach that culture.

UNDERSTANDING CULTURE

Postmodernism and the discussions surrounding it attempt to take a hard look at the culture we live in. Culture is both good and bad, beautiful and ugly, directive and reflective. Culture is what we grow up in.

Some urban churches simply see culture as "the world," interpreting culture negatively as something we must save urban youth from at all costs. I've heard many urban church folks use the phrase "in the world" to characterize their life before becoming a Christian. I used to use the term myself, but I wonder now if it is actually biblically appropriate. I know the Scripture that talks about "being in the world but not of it," but "being in the world" as a synonym for living a life of sin seems misguided. Could it be that this language hinders our ability to see "the world" and the culture around us as something we should engage for kingdom purposes? When the urban church takes a stance against "the world," it tends not to take time to understand culture, its influences, and how God might be already present there as we attempt to bring the gospel of Jesus Christ to young people.

Until recently most of my urban ministry experience has been in parachurch organizations, trying to reach unchurched youth right where they are. This meant going to the high school campus, the park and the mall, or simply hanging out on the block. It also meant taking time to examine and observe culture as Paul did in Athens (Acts 17). To be effective in this kind of ministry, I couldn't afford to simply paint culture as the enemy. In the parachurch setting, those attempting to reach unchurched urban youth with high-risk issues realize that they have to spend a lot of time in "secular" culture. Much effort goes into meeting youth where they are, just as Jesus met the Samaritan woman at the well (John 4). So connecting to, observing and understanding urban culture has become a natural part of how I do ministry.

Urban youth workers often have more opportunities to reach unchurched youth in a parachurch organization than they have in a local church, simply because of the theology of culture the churches have. In the urban church, the focus tends to be on ministry to youth already in the church by creating a junior church modeled on the activities of adults in the church. No wonder it can be a challenge to develop a church-based ministry model for examining, observing and reaching urban young people within a hip-hop, postmodern, urban culture.

TRAITS OF POSTMODERNITY

But can contemporary urban culture be described as postmodern? If yes, might hip-hop culture and the elements of African American culture within it be the best lenses through which to understand postmodernity in the urban context?

The following list of significant traits of postmodern culture does not encompass all the elements of and issues surrounding postmodernity, but these traits can help us draw some connections between it and urban culture:

- a culture of questioning everything
- a culture where truth is relative
- a culture where relationships mean more than institutions
- a culture that values storytelling
- a culture of emotion and experience

Some of the traits on this list are congruent with urban culture and others don't match up perfectly. For instance, "relationships mean more than institutions" may be questionable because many institutions still have a strong influence among young people in urban communities—for example, the Urban League, the NAACP, the black church, the Catholic Church and various community centers. On the other hand, hip-hop culture through rap is a great example of "a culture that values storytelling."

WHO IS AT THE TABLE?

Now, I realize that urban culture includes ethnicities beyond the African American ethnic group and many subcultures beyond hip-hop. But the broader culture we live in is larger than postmodernism too, and my point here is to connect postmodernism to urban culture in order to broaden and diversify the discussions I've witnessed over the past couple of years around culture, Christianity and the church. I'm concerned that those participating in and influencing discussions, events and books centered on the church and culture tend to be predominantly white and male. They also almost always take place outside the setting of the inner city, despite the fact that white teens *especially outside the city* tend to be influenced by inner-city culture. Church youth, regardless of ethnicity, are influenced by hip-hop:

> Of interest is the finding that about half of all born-again teens purchased some rap or hip-hop recordings within the past year. Of related interest is the fact that most teenagers' parents have no idea what music their kids listen to or the lyrical content of their musical diet. Given the importance of music in shaping the values and ideals of our young people, we would be well advised to devote greater attention to this dimension of our youths' development.
>
> (GEORGE BARNA, *REAL TEENS*)

As we talk about postmodern culture and its influence, we are remiss when we don't include hip-hop culture as urban postmodernism or recognize its influence beyond the urban area. As it is, postmodernism discussions in many Christian conferences may be limited, as Michael Eric Dyson suggests in his book *Open Mike:* "Is postmodernism just modernism in drag?" That is, sometimes the postmodern discussion among emerging Christian leaders consists mainly of young whites who grew up in the modern church complaining about what they don't like about their daddy's church. It is white folks talking about white church, white Jesus and white theology. What's more, given that these discussions are mostly taking place outside the inner city, those around the table tend to overrepresent the socially privileged. If this is true, it's nothing new to the urban community and or to people of color in America. We are very aware that Christianity in America has largely been shaped by a dominant and privileged culture. But those who are discussing shifts in the church and culture need to be aware of it too.

HIP-HOP AS POSTMODERN

Now let's look at hip-hop culture as postmodern culture. Though I treat hip-hop here as a subculture of urban culture, its influence has spread beyond the confines of the city. It has risen from its inner-city roots to influence youth from the American suburbs to Tokyo. As the top consumers of its music, white teenage males in America do a great job of keeping hip-hop culture in business. Today it's not a shock to see a suburban white teenage male wearing the hip-hop fashion label FUBU, even though this clothing line's African American creators specified that the letters mean "For Us, by Us." Their race-specific approach doesn't stop whites from choosing "black only" clothes. It hasn't kept Latinos or Southeast Asians from being hip-hop consumers either.

Hip-hop as a culture, though having a global influence, must also be viewed in direct connection to the culture of postsoul, post-civil rights black youth:

> those African-Americans born between 1965 and 1984 who came of age in the eighties and nineties and who share a specific set of values and attitudes. At the core are our thoughts about family, relationships child rearing, career, racial identity, race relations, and politics. Collectively, these

views make up a complex worldview that has not been correctly defined.

This worldview first began to be expressed in the insightful
mid- to late 1980's sociopolitical critiques of rap artists like
NWA, KRS-One, Poor Righteous Teachers, Queen Latifah,
and others. . . . Collectively, hip-hop generation writers, artists, filmmakers, activists, and scholars like these laid the
foundation for understanding our generation's worldview.

(BAKARI KITWANA, THE HIP HOP GENERATION)

Let's explore how the traits of postmodernism listed earlier
tie into hip-hop culture. In regard to *questioning everything,* hip-
hop culture and its music in particular question everything from
whether the American dream is attainable for urban youth to
whether the police force and the national government are systems that can be trusted.

I once asked a young man involved in my youth ministry about
why he listened to "gangsta rap." His response was "They say
things about the police that I believe are true. I'm tired of the way
police treat black youth."

It disturbs me on a number of levels that a young person in the
church would feel that gangsta rap does a more adequate job of expressing tensions and stereotypes regarding the police in relation
to urban youth than do the church and other community organizations. Unfortunately, gangsta rap does not provide a positive solution, unless one harks back to the 1960s and 1970s and believes
that the Black Panther way of taking up arms is the proper solution.

Gangsta rap is not the only genre that questions the police and
other authority figures and institutions; such questioning shows
up in consciousness rap as well. Public Enemy's song "Fight the
Power" comes to mind. The classic "The Message" by Grandmaster Flash and Grandmaster Melle Mel questions the ability of

youth to live without losing their heads on the streets of the inner city dealing day to day with broken glass, drug pushers, prostitution and the smell of urine.

In its double CD release *Speakerboxx/The Love Below,* Outkast questions hip-hop itself and where it has come with its many lyrics and video images glorifying the gangster lifestyle and its loss of a more intellectual and creative spirit. On one of the two CDs in this project, emcee Andre totally abandons rap as we know it to use styles of jazz, rock and soul, questioning what comes to people's minds when they think hip-hop.

Hip-hop culture puts many things in a dominant Westernized society as well as its own cultural evolution to the question. In politics, figures such as the Reverends Al Sharpton and Jesse Jackson have questioned the truth behind the claims and platforms of the two major political parties. They then opened themselves up to questions and criticism by going through divorce and having a child out of wedlock, respectively. Martin Luther King Jr. in his "I Have a Dream" speech questioned if America was truly living up to its Declaration of Independence. In many ways all of this is about whether in the United States there's one truth for people of privilege and another for the less privileged.

The civil rights movement, the black power movement, the Nation of Islam and liberation theology are roots of the hip-hop movement that publicly questioned the Christianity, the democracy and the pluralism of American society. These roots have played some part, I believe, in the political activism that you now see within the hip-hop movement. It's P. Diddy on *106 and Park* on BET leading a "Vote or Die" campaign in 2004. It's the Hip-Hop Summit Action Network started by Russell Simmons and others, who in an article in the June 2004 issue of *XXL* magazine said,

> Straight up! We are building a mass youth movement. We are not just demanding change with our voices, music, art,

and high aspirations. Collectively, we are also taking action
and being responsible for the motivation and encouragement of youthful soldiers in the war against poverty and ignorance. Spittin' truth in the face of injustice is an obligation.
("HIP-HOP SUMMIT: TAKING BACK RESPONSIBILITY")

Ben Chavis, a former pastor and NAACP president is a key
front leader of this movement. The context of the inner city and
the issues, barriers and challenges, that go with growing up there
play a major role in the questioning as well as action of hip-hop
culture. Rap music, then, is more than either party music or degrading music. "Rap music is much more than a series of clever
rhymes set to a drum beat and music. It is a reflection of how
young Black Americans perceive their place in the dominant society" (Bob Hepburn, "Rap Music: Give Me My Respect, Man!" *Urban Mission,* September 1992).

Connected to questioning everything is *a culture where truth is
relative.* Hip-hop in its young history (birthdate 1974, the Bronx,
New York) has questioned many things lifted up in American history and pop culture as truth. Hip-hop has questioned if Elvis is
the king of rock and roll or if he really just stole and profited off
black music and style at a time when African Americans in the
South weren't accepted as mainstream rock idols. Again, beginning in the 1960s and 1970s, questions arose about American
Christianity's impact on the African American community. In past
decades the clear majority of African Americans would have been
considered Christian, but with the questioning brought on by the
Nation of Islam, which led to religious questioning in hip-hop
through the development of the Five Percent Nation, and even the
questioning of James Cone through liberation theology, a relativ-
ist view of truth and God has developed and is seen clearly within
hip-hop.

The Five Percent Nation, which grew out of the Nation of Islam, has over time become an alternative religion of hip-hop and street culture. In a contribution to *Everything but the Burden,* edited by hip-hop writer Greg Tate, Melvin Gibbs says this about the history of the Five Percent Nation:

This modern thug's metaphysics comes from the group commonly known as the Five Percenters. It was started in 1964 by Clarence 13X Smith, a former member of the Nation of Islam, who is known to his followers as Father Allah. . . . The term "Five Percenter" is derived from the Lost and Found Muslim Lessons, which were written in the form of questions posed by Fard Muhammad, the founder of the NOI, and answered by Elijah Muhammad. One of the questions Fard asked was "Who are the five percent?" Elijah explained that the five percent were the percentage of the population that were, "poor righteous teachers," those who knew and understood the "true" knowledge of God.

("THUGGODS: SPIRITUAL DARKNESS AND HIP-HOP")

Why do I think it important to know this alternative spirituality? Only in recent years has there been preaching and writing that has not only challenged a Eurocentric Christianity but also presented an alternative view that is more multicultural and in some cases more authentic. Some of these voices, such as James Cone, Tom Skinner, John Perkins, Martin Luther King Jr. and Renita Weems, were those of professed Christians seeking to dismantle a Eurocentric Christianity. But others have sought to present an alternative Afrocentric religion separate from Christianity. The Nation of Islam and others within the African American community were questioning if Christianity was truly the religion of the African American.

It should not surprise us, then, that this challenging within and outside of Eurocentric Christianity has showed up within hip-hop culture. Groups and solo emcees such as Public Enemy, KRS-ONE, Poor Righteous Teachers, the Last Asiatic Disciples and X-Clan have used their rap to attempt to bring spiritual and educational awareness. We also see this today in rappers such as Mos Def, Talib Kweli, the Roots and Dead Prez. I believe this style of rap is influenced by the Nation of Islam, the Five Percent Nation, political groups of the 1960s and 1970s such as the Black Panthers and the Last Poets, and even the Christian black preaching tradition in America.

You see a mixture of Islam, Christianity and New Age within hip-hop culture. Today we could very well be in a postblack church culture, as many in the African American urban community look to other places besides the black church for a sense of spiritual truth. Add to this the number of African and Asian immigrants coming to the cities of the United States, bringing with them other cultural values and religious beliefs outside of Christianity.

Various multicultural coalitions are also contributing to the relativizing of truth. It's very normal to see a black preacher, a white lesbian activist, a rabbi and a Latino union worker marching together down a city street, protesting for liberation. You would think their various takes on truth would make this kind of postmodern freedom march impossible, but it seems as if in the urban community there is a way to bring people of faith together with people of goodwill around issues of social justice. Hip-hop culture has an influence as well as a tolerance that brings disparate people groups together. Hip-hop culture tends to swing toward the liberal side politically; this could be partly because the liberal political agenda seems more receptive to multiculturalism than does the conservative political agenda. A more liberal political agenda seems to lead to a relative stance on truth, with a high regard for multicultural tolerance. This is a challenge for the Christian, who should be clear based on Scripture about Jesus as "the way, the truth and the life."

The third trait of postmodernity listed above is that *relationships mean more than institutions.* Rapper Kanye West markets himself as a college dropout, challenging the notion of needing an institution's diploma to be considered an intellectual. On his single "Jesus Walks," he spits out lyrics that present him as both an intellectual and a theologian though he has no seminary degree or ordination certificate. I don't mention this to say that I agree with his theology, but many black preachers in fact seem to find success as pastors based on their relationship with the listeners to their sermons rather than from having received a degree from an institution.

In part this reflects a deeper issue: not all African Americans feel that they can trust a predominantly white institution of higher learning. I grew up believing that it was important to go to college because that was what you needed to do to get a job that paid well, not because my parents had a high regard for college as an important institution. Many African American parents prepare their children to deal with predominantly white institutions by teaching an "eat the fish and spit out the bones" mentality. When I decided to enter seminary to work toward a master's degree, some African Americans questioned why I would attend the institution.

This is not to say that the African American community does not trust education, but that historically it has wrestled with certain institutions that are predominantly white. The first phase of this wrestling involved winning the right to gain entrance into these institutions, such as schools, restaurants, social clubs and corporate jobs. The next phase of wrestling has involved questioning what there is to gain in the larger society by being involved in these institutions. I've spent a great deal of my life dealing with predominantly white institutions, and I must say that one of my survival tactics has been to build relationships with other African Americans within those institutions. I struggled my freshman year at St. John's University in Collegeville, Minnesota, but rooming with Lee Lindsey, an African American, helped me get through. This relationship was valuable in helping me deal with the institution.

The relationship value shows up in the sports realm as well. Many urban African Americans leave college early to go to the NBA, hoping they can provide better for family and friends. Relationships are key in this culture over loyalty to an institution. You cannot separate the issues, barriers and challenges of growing up in inner-city culture from this valuing of relationships over institutions.

Street gangs within inner-city settings are another striking example of the influence and power of relationships. Gangsta rap plays strong to this culture, and it's the major reason that gangsta rap is anti-institution and antiauthority.

In regarding to *valuing the power of storytelling,* the first mainstream rap smash single "Rapper's Delight" is storytelling par excellence. This element of hip-hop culture reflects its roots of African culture. Because enslaved African Americans were denied book-based education, the oral tradition of storytelling was an essential survival tool for passing on knowledge, culture and religion to the next generation. This rich tradition of storytelling continues today within hip-hop culture through rap and spoken word. Hiphop has used rap to tell stories of urban youth, poverty, oppression, inner-city life, anger and African American history. Some have called rappers the news reporters of the ghetto. Another evidence of this storytelling value is the resurgence of poetry in hiphop culture through spoken word poetry, mixed at times with neosoul rhythms.

All of these contemporary versions of storytelling have roots as well in the tradition of storytelling within black preaching. Martin Luther King Jr., Gardner Taylor and Caesar Clark will go down in history as great preachers because of their gift of storytelling. I will deal in more depth with the connection between rapping (emceeing) and the black preaching tradition in a later chapter.

Finally, postmodernity is a culture of *emotion and experience.* True hip-hop is not just about being heard; it's about being felt. Hip-hop is the emotion of L.L. Cool J. rapping with his shirt off, covered with sweat. It's the experience of a hip-hop concert crowd "waving their hands in the air, like they just don't care." It's the emotion after a Kevin Garnett slam-dunk. It's the visual experience of break dancing in the streets. It's the experience of street basketball at Rucker Park or the And 1 Tour at a local arena. It's the experience of seeing Randy Moss catch a touchdown. It's the emotion of the follow-up end-zone celebration dance. Hip-hop is about the low-end bass coming out of the speaker and hitting you in the chest. What is being rapped to you is what someone has really lived. Hip-hop is about giving suburban youth an experience of urban life.

Now I would be the first to say that sometimes what is depicted as the urban experience on BET and MTV is full of stereotypes and less than authentic, but even viewing that is an experience in itself. (By the way, BET stands for Black Entertainment Television, but today the corporation isn't owned by blacks at all; black businessman and NBA team owner Robert Johnson sold it to Viacom.) I would compare it to professional wrestling. You know it's fake, but boy, can it still draw a crowd as well as ratings! And when it comes to experience and emotion, hip-hop doesn't stop with rap music; it moves to the screen with movies like *Juice, Boyz in the Hood* and *Training Day.* The emotion and experience of hip-hop is truly multisensory.

Hip-hop culture and its historically African American elements, then, provide a a urban take on postmodernism. From here the next step is to use this conclusion to follow the lead of groups like the Emergent Village and create discussion forums around the church and culture. If hip-hop is indeed a great way to peek into what is influencing urban youth, the urban church must ask itself what it's going to do about that. If hip-hop has replaced the church as the anchor of the urban community, then the urban church must wrestle with how it will work to reclaim urban youth. The urban church can no longer afford to paint the culture as the enemy but instead must raise up its own emerging leaders, willing to pioneer a movement that will reach urban youth within their culture. This will take building alliances and taking on elements of hip-hop culture as evangelistic and discipleship tools. That entails a whole rethinking of the urban church, practically and theologically.

5

Hip-Hop THEOLOGY

Music is spiritual! This will come as no surprise to an avid music listener. The music of artists such as the late great Sam Cooke, whose melodic sound stirred women's hearts to shout praises to God, even though some of these same women were trying to sleep with Sam, brought about a spiritual connection. When you are in church, especially a church in the city, music is a key element in any service. If the music is banging, the service was a "success." Through music an emotional connection can occur on a Sunday morning between the soloist and those in the congregation over what God has brought or is bringing them through: shared experiences of hope, pain, injustice and restoration. No matter what else happens in the service, the choir, the soloist, the trio or the youth choir better bring the funk with whatever they are singing, or the pastor will get a call on Monday.

Music is power because music comes from an artist's subjective life experiences, and those experiences influence and stimulate thoughts and ideologies in the minds of others. The artist's reflection on his or her life creates and shapes a perspective on life that others can and do identify with. When you delve into the history of any people group, you cannot separate that history from what the people sing about. This is the key principle for our exploration here and the reason why theological probing must be done in order to grasp hip-hop theology, which is the study of God in hip-hop culture and how God or spirituality is understood. The following general definition of spirituality does not specify a particular religion or faith; it is from Mike Dyson, speaking at St. Sabina Catholic Church in 1999: "Spirituality is sustaining one's sanity in the midst of cultural conflict while pressing toward a moral goal that is highly unachievable yet still possible in order to sustain one's spirituality, creating a social balance to live another day." People today will often say, "I'm spiritual but not religious," thus separating themselves from a religious institution or system (most often the church). What they mean but are not saying is "This institution will not enslave me—they don't understand and are too judgmental, hypocritical and fake." They claim a more individual spirituality: "I have my own understanding of God that works for me."

Now, if we can use this description without tagging it as New Age or any other cultic script, then we can swim into the waters of hip-hop spirituality. When missionaries go to the country they are going to serve, they study the culture, language, religion, school system and overall way of life of the targeted people group without any judgment. So it should be as we begin to explore hip-hop's spirituality. We must not look suspiciously around every corner and demonize what we are uncomfortable with or what does not fit into our theological bent. We must rise above this kind of reaction if we are to gain understanding, or else we will never hear a word anyone, especially in hip-hop, has to say about themselves.

The first thing that must be washed out of our heads is that Africans became Christians after they came to America. The assumption is common that whites freed Africans from their demonic religious ways when they were brought to America and became Christians. When a certain group has taught you a history for so long that you go to sleep on it as if it were the gospel, but then new information is given to you, you don't know what to do.

We don't have time to unpack all the story of the Ethiopian Orthodox Church, which was founded in the fourth century A.D. and is one of the oldest in Christendom. It is second only to the Coptic Church of Egypt, and both of these churches existed before slavery and led the way for European and American churches in ministry. So according to history, Africans were worshiping Christ long before Africans were stolen from their homelands and enslaved, despite the assumption that it was white slave owners and abolitionists who started churches among the oppressed African slaves.

Tradition holds that the preaching of St. Mark brought the gospel to Egypt and that the first Egyptian conversions happened within a large Jewish community in Alexandria. In February 1976, the Confession of Alexandria was issued by the general committee of the All African Conference of Churches, recognizing the priority of the churches of Egypt and Ethiopia. Psalm 68:31, which speaks of how Egypt will bring gifts and Ethiopia will "stretch its hands to God," was indeed prophetic.

Today there are over 375 million Christians in Africa, and they didn't all result from the ministry of missionaries from the West. The oldest Christian school in the world is the Catechetical School of Alexandria. Christian thought has long been influenced by theologians from Egypt, especially Alexandria. St. Augustine of Hippo, Africa (north), was very influential with teaching and building up the students with theology and practical living for Christ. So within the African American experience from slavery till now there have been deep roots of faith in Christ, inside of an African cultural experience. In fact, the African way of life has always been one of spirituality and oneness with God.

To understand the spirituality of hip-hop, we must begin to grasp the intense quest of an oppressed people for a window of hope that can sustain life in the midst of crazy paradoxes. In fact, hope is all around the oppressed, however hidden it might be behind the struggles that we face. Hopelessness and resilience can coexist amongst an oppressed people through the generations, passed down from child to child and from generation to generation. So reader, put down all your evangelical guns as I seek to describe what exists in the real world of hip-hop.

HIP-HOP AND LIBERATION

Hip-hop spirituality has connections to liberation theology. In liberation theology, salvation involves deliverance from oppression. The obstacle to such salvation is the cycle of oppression and exploitation of the powerless by the powerful.

Self-awareness liberation theology. This liberation type of theology is manifested in two consistent themes or stages in hip-hop. First is self-awareness. This stage is like Solomon's perspective in the book of Ecclesiastes when he says, "Utterly meaningless! Everything is meaningless" (1:2). It's the feeling of *This is all life can bring* after trying unsuccessfully to find satisfaction and peace. Hip-hop liberation is found in personal self-awareness when an emcee is spitting about a place of personal reflection and affirms that new decisions must be made for a destructive cycle to stop. At this point, what one learned in the past, often about God, is questioned along with the authority behind it—the church, pastors, the Bible and even the grandmomma who brought one to church. The questions arise from the realization that not enough freedom was given in church or from awareness of the "churchianity" that was constructed in order to build ownership in what was being taught. When the young adult gets hit by the ways of the world, he concludes that Mom's faith or Grandma's faith in this Christianity was only for their generation because it does not seem to fit with his current situation. This expression is often brought about not through violence, jail or criminal activity but through a personal crossroads experience—maybe a brush with death, having a child, falling in love, sickness or a spiritual awakening.

On Common's CD *One Day It Will All Make Sense,* he says in "G.O.D (Gaining One's Definition)": "Told to believe in Christ because for me he did die / but never ever given a reason for why / so curiosity killed the catechism / it's the Bible and the Quran / you got to read em boyz you can't just skim em." His critique is embarrassingly true: the church tells everyone to believe in Jesus because he died for you, which is true, but it has never provided an apologetic for this truth to build sustainability. When life happens to these young believers and they reach back to grab the faith that they were "told to believe in," it is gone because they never owned it. When they asked serious questions, they were judged to be rebellious or just plain difficult and were given empty answers.

There is a gap in the current generation that is not hip-hop's fault, even though hip-hop doesn't solve it: a separation between what you believe and how you behave, between what you know and how you live. You find that the gap is accepted as long you acknowledge that there is a higher power. What hip-hop articulates in the self-discovery phase of its expression of liberation theology is that there is something missing that is not understood, that is a cosmic relationship, a relationship with Christ. Ecclesiastes 3:11 states that we have "eternality of Spirit," which means we have this hole in our heart, and we try to fill it with everything except Christ. Hip-hop's self-awareness recognizes *only* that something is missing; it does not recognize what it is and where it can be found. The church is the last place it would look for the answer.

Mos Def said it this way: "If hip-hop ain't gonna get better until the people get better, well, what is going to help the people get better? When people understand that they are valuable and they are not valuable because they have a lot of money or somebody thinks they sexy but because they have been created by God, and God thinks you're valuable, whether or not you recognize that value."

Restoration liberation theology. The other phase of liberation theology expressed in hip-hop is *restoration* or a feeling of loss of self due to living life on one's own terms and reaching a dead end. It's like the prodigal son's pig-pen experience in the book of Luke. He lived life on his own terms and it came back to bite him. But eventually he sought restoration and went home (Luke 15:11-32). We must extract the content of the message of what the artists are saying about emptiness, anger, money, and replace the content with what Christ seeks for us to know about such issues. Our learning about what is going on in hip-hop and the needs that this culture is facing can often be found through hip-hop's lyrics. Once we have bottomed out, we long for something, someone—God— to heal us and make things right.

One expression of such restoration can be seen in a music video by DMX called "Angel," from his *Great Depression* CD. The video pictures a young man who is trying to find meaning in drug dealing and violence. His life on the street leads him to prison. When he comes out, he wants to be restored and seeks fulfillment in rap with the skills he has. But as his career starts to blow up (that means "to do well"), he is chased by an angel of death who tries to destroy his life. The death angel catches him and tries to kill him at the door of a church, but just in time an angel from heaven comes to save him. Now he crawls into the church, and a child comes to him and says, "Stand up and walk" (an echo of Scripture's words "And a little child shall lead them" [Isaiah 11:6]). After all his attempts to find restoration by himself, the church proves to be the only place to find real restoration. DMX starts to pray to Jesus and finally experiences completeness. We in the church need to open our ears and hear that need for restoration; our refusal to do so has been the church's shame. We have embraced those who we're comfortable embracing according to certain sins—but what about those we're not comfortable with? Are we really ready to model restoration as Christ has for us?

These expressions of self-awareness liberation theology and restoration liberation theology in hip-hop can be doorways through which the church can bridge the gap and bring a clear message of the gospel.

WHILE THE CHURCH SLEEPS

The African American church experience does value restoration. If there is any place that will truly accept you back just the way you are, no matter what you've done, it is the African American congregation. The desire to welcome you and to have you "come as you are" to the African American worship experience, however, is coupled with a weakness in practical application to build sustainable faith. It is true that the U.S. church as a whole has this flaw, but in the African American church we mostly have great preaching institutions rather than real, hands-on, life-changing ministry.

The complication with the African American congregation in relation to hip-hop is that the church is void of solid youth ministry programming. Typically, there is one youth day a year, presided over by Reverend Johnson, who is so far removed from youth that his message is irrelevant. The junior ushers, junior preachers, junior elders and junior everything for this one day make up the entire youth program. There are no empowering ministry components that would bring holistic deliverance to the lives of students. Hip-hop brings juice to the life of a student—juice right now—empowerment and the sense that they are important.

What the church does is to teach *at* the students, assuming that they understand. Because they quote a few verses or sing in the choir the church thinks that they are serious about their walk with Christ. But just the opposite is true: most students cover up their issues because they know that they can't be real in the church.

Acts 19:13 tells of the seven sons of Sceva, who went out and were healing people in the name of Jesus. They came to a demon-possessed man and said to him, "In the name of Jesus who Paul preaches, we command you to come out!" Here is where things flipped on them. The demon-possessed man said, "Paul I know and Jesus I know, but yo behind I don't know." And the Bible records that the demons beat the young men until they left them crib-naked and bleeding.

See, what happens in the life of young people is that the church is not really ready to go deeper with them into the areas of life that don't fit nice and neat in a church context. So when a temptation hits the life of a kid, they come at it like the seven sons of Sceva and say, "In the name of Jesus who my preacher talks about or who my Sunday school teacher talks about, I tell you to leave!" But because Christ is not living in them, because they only know *about* Jesus, they get beat down by the temptation, and after a while they think that sin is just a way of life.

When Boquintella gets pregnant, suddenly the church is all in an uproar. But when did the church talk about sex and help her and others understand sexual pressure and provide a way of escape in order that she could live a sexually pure life?

African American students today are locked in a room with the doors open. They are emancipated but not free. On June 19, 1865, in Galveston, Texas, Union soldiers came to tell the slaves that they were free. You see, the Emancipation Proclamation had been issued on January 1, 1863, a whole two and a half years earlier, but the black people of Galveston didn't know about it till 1965.

The church that does not help students to comprehend the life, death and life again of Jesus Christ in a very real and practical way is part of the problem rather than the solution. What an indictment on the church that we have the power of God through his Son Jesus Christ yet fall short because we esteem tradition over life change.

The spirituality hip-hop offers is attractive but can't provide consistent, holistic solutions—internal peace and sustainable life change. Like all other musical styles, hip-hop is spiritual by nature; however, its influence depends on the artist and his or her interpretation of life. And it would be putting too much weight on hip-hop to expect it to meet all the spiritual needs of its people.

The African American church's teachings on the deity of Christ and his powerful attributes as well as on the social ills that confront us and how God can and will deliver us were what ushered in the civil rights movement. (Civil rights, of course, were a reaction rather than a solution.) These teachings have always been a significant component of African American congregational life. The African American church has always tended to be conservative theologically but liberal in regard to social issues. There is an intertwining of these two that can cause confusion about the ministry of the African American worship experience, whose message is both for the individual and for the community.

The church in the African American community used to consistently respond to and seek to fulfill this verse as a scriptural mandate: "He has told you, O man, what is good; / And what does the LORD require of you / But to do justice, to love kindness, / And to walk humbly with your God? / The voice of the LORD will call to the city" (Micah 6:8-9). Unfortunately, over the last couple of decades a shift has occurred as more and more preaching focuses on a God who wants you to prosper materially. As congregations pursue this God out, pastors swell up with twin Bentleys and diamond earrings. Meanwhile the hip-hop community laughs and guides a generation to what is real.

The lack of teaching about a Christ who understands our needs, who was tempted yet didn't sin, and who overcame the obstacles we face with authority and power creates a separation between us and God, who understands all that we face. The void of teaching that this Christ was incarnational will continue to keep hope away from those who are seeking to understand God. Tupac sought to express this in his cut "Black Jesuz." He talks about how this Jesuz hurts like thugs hurt and hangs out with those involved in illegal activity. Even the change of z replacing s is his attempt to help others see Jesus as incarnational. This Jesus is a saint who is not worshiped behind closed doors in the building of a church but is worshiped every day on the block. Tupac's cut screams out that we need to see, hear and realize that God has not forgotten us, that he cares and understands yet has a better way if we trust him. People who are too busy criticizing Tupac and hip-hop will not see the value in using this as a bridge with someone who is looking for clarity about Jesus

The gospel according to hip-hop is a message of justice and power. Too often the church has failed to be proactive in communities that lack sufficient economic, health and other resources. Justice is not just a Christian thing, it is a humanity thing. This is one point of connection to spark conversation between the church and the hip-hop community.

A BIBLICAL—AND CURRENT—MESS

Genesis 12:10-20 pictures a dilemma like the one that young people today often face in relation to the system and the need for someone to stand up for justice. Abram is following an unknown God, and as he is obeying this God's call to move his family and leave his country, the place they land undergoes a famine. Abram decides to go to Egypt to survive. Once there, knowing that his wife, Sarai, is fine and that the king of Egypt may kill him just to take her, he tells Sarai to tell the king that she is his sister. Believing she *is* his sister, the king soon starts giving Abram male servants, maidservants, money, donkeys, cows and other props because Sarai is so beautiful. So Abram has devised a plan to get over on the corrupt system, and it is working.

Now here hypocrisy comes into the story. The king and his court start to get boils. They start tripping about what is going on, and they find out that Sarai is married to Abram. So they come to Abram and say to him that he was wrong for lying and saying that this woman was his sister when she is really his wife.

The question is who was really in the wrong. The king has created a corrupt system, but when his corrupt system is found out and it gets jammed, he wants to blame those he oppressed for doing wrong. Or is it Abram who is wrong, because he understood this system and decided to work it in order to just live another day? What about how Sarai was used as a tool to negotiate freedom and power between two men?

Let's look at this in a twenty-first-century light. Say there are two minority high school students. One attends a school in the city, where 5,200 dollars per student is apportioned to the school district annually, and the other attends a school in a nearby suburb, where 10,000 to 12,000 is apportioned to educate each kid. The city student plays sports; he notices that he's not allowed to take any books home, yet the basketball team has new gym bags, new shoes, and transportation to and from each game. The student in the suburban school gets to take books home, and he plays sports also.

Both students have a 3.8 GPA, and both are at the top of their class. They both graduate on time and attend the University of Illinois. But soon the student from the city, who plays on the U of I basketball team, starts having a hard time in math class. The kid from the burbs is his classmate there. It turns out that the student who is playing ball can't read at college level and may lose his scholarship if he does not pass his courses. The system that was corrupt from the beginning now, just like the king in Genesis, acts self-righteous and exposes the boy's reading problem. But the same system regularly chooses to put new shoes on a kid's feet for playing ball rather than a book in his hand to succeed.

Two themes that are common to the Christian church and hip-hop speak to these issues: not only the need for justice but also our human struggle and pain. Hip-hop delivers hard-hitting messages about both. Sadly, the church has lost a way to explain Jesus to a culture that is wide open to the truth of Christ.

The absence of teaching about the humanity of Jesus hinders hip-hop heads, as they assume that Christianity does not connect to real life. It is in Jesus' incarnation that we can connect to his deity—in the reality that Jesus got mad, was poor, dealt with ridicule and disdain. If there is not solid teaching on the humanity of Christ, we see him as a God who is supposed to fix stuff in our life but not a God who can empathize with temptation we face. This failure in the church's teaching of Christ makes more attractive hip-hop's claim to the physical, mental and emotional toil of life with self-knowledge, as well as the Black Muslims' confrontation of life challenges and social issues. Again, this is one reason hip-hop doesn't always fit in with the church: the church tends to skirt the issues brought up by hip-hop.

Among all worship styles and ministry approaches, those of the African American congregation should be the on the front lines of change. Now, make no mistake, African American congregations *have* helped bring about social change for the cause of Christ, but in the world of hip-hop the African American worship experience is a joke. Busta Rhymes on his video *Make It Clap* walks into a black church and goes up to the pulpit to talk with the pastor—whose name, by the way, is Pastor Offering. He asks for a blessing, and the pastor replies, "That blessing is gonna cost you about 100,000 dollars!" Busta looks at him dumbfounded. This is how we in the African American worship experience come off to hip-hop: as irrelevant, unapproachable, always begging for money, self-seeking and having no power that represents the God we preach about.

One of the most prominent religious expressions that has arisen from hip-hop is the Five Percent Nation. Knowledge of self is the consistent theme within its teaching. The Nation warns that 85 percent of people walk through life deaf, dumb and blind; 10 percent are bloodsuckers of the poor; and only 5 percent know the truth. Its members state that they are gods and use Psalm 82:4-8 as the foundational Scripture to support this belief. One of the major leaders of the Five Percent Nation was Rakim (an acronym for Ruler, Allah, Kingdom, Eye or Islam, Master). Other prophets of this teaching or a similar type of teaching have included KRS-ONE, Poor Righteous Teachers, Brand Nubian, Busta Rhymes and Public Enemy.

The teaching of the Five Percent Nation reflects the larger drive of hip-hop: the need to be self-supporting, self-educating and self directed. The statements of Five Percent Nation adherents often carries a compelling force, for they are very serious about what they are studying and able to explain and defend it.

The Five Percent teaching is clearly in conflict with sound Christian theology, but unfortunately most of us Christians are so lame that all we do in response is quote some preacher, some book we read or some cliché. I believe we could present a much better defense of our faith if we spent time unpacking the Word of God with young people and gained knowledge of the African presence in the Bible and the powerful ways God moved in the early church in Africa. There needs to be a hip-hop apologetic for the Christian faith—not spitting out quotes from a sermon or repeating what your cousin or your friend told you the day before yesterday, but a serious understanding of biblical truth and how it speaks to hip-hop questions. As followers of Christ, there is no reason we should not be able to give a defense of our faith.

We need to approach hip-hoppers with an awareness that hip-hop is marked by a distinct consciousness and a desire to discuss spiritual issues and to bring this culture to a better place. We must come not with Euro-evangelical prejudgment but with an open heart and mind to bring to hip-hop culture a better, clearer understanding of what it means to be a follower of Christ. Actually the strongest testimony we can have in the hip-hop culture is not what we say but what we do and how we do it.

"Refuse the awful temptation to scale down your dreams to the level of the event which is your immediate experience." This call by Howard Thurman aptly expresses our challenge as Christ followers as we seek to create connections with those of this generation whose dreams of a better life are bigger than the temptation to get pregnant, smoke weed or join a gang. Hip-hop though rap makes this connect, even if it can't fulfill its promise. When will we wake up and flip the script?

Part Three

Bringing Hip-Hop
INTO YOUR CHURCH

6

Holy Hip-Hop

Hip-hop can be holy! My friend Fred Lynch has created a hip-hop version of the Gospel of John, *The Epic.* Fred is truly a hip-hop theologian, using hip-hop street language to make the Word of God relevant for this generation without watering down its ancient message. Here's a sample from John 1:1-5:

> In the beginning was the Word, the manifest logic of heard—
> unblurred shining from the inner sanctum of the Third.
> Unbroken catastrophical quotes spoken
> from the essence of eternity's original notion.
> All things were made by His motion
> and without Him was no-thing brought to being,
> all matter engrossed Him.
> In Him was life and that life was the light of men,
> shining in the dark but darkness didn't comprehend.
>
> (THE EPIC: A HIP HOP VERSION OF THE GOSPEL OF JOHN)

Holy Hip-Hop is rap music created specifically to glorify Jesus Christ and bring the good news of Jesus Christ to those who are living in and influenced by hip-hop culture. Now this is just a definition that I am offering; you may hear others as you venture further into this music genre, subculture and ministry opportunity. Some involved in Holy Hip-Hop probably have yet to define what it is that they are doing. Many likely started out loving hip-hop, became Christian, and now are simply putting Jesus lyrics with their artistic gift and passion. In any case, the existence of Holy Hip-Hop is a great opportunity for the church to embrace the emerging generation and create new ministry methods for advancing the church's mission. Ambassador writes in his "Apologetics" song on the *Christology* CD: "I live and die for what I believe in, / Represent truth of God's Word every season. / Since I'm the reason for His bleedin', / Now I represent Him til the day I stop breathin'."

This style of rap music ought to be embraced by the church for a couple of reasons. One, Holy Hip-Hop can be used as an evangelism and outreach tool. Second, young people who are gifted in the arts, especially those with gifts of dance, spoken word or art with the spray can, ought to be nurtured within the church so that they realize how to use their God-given gifts to glorify the Gift Giver. Sadly, many Holy Hip-Hop artists have a hard time getting support from the church. But others point back to the church as the place that allowed them to develop gifts for kingdom advancement that otherwise would have been used in a negative way.

My hope is that as you read this chapter you will be inspired, if you are not already, to use elements of hip-hop culture to create your own Holy Hip-Hop ministry. I will present some models in this chapter, and other models will surface in later chapters as we look at how to start a hip-hop church. This chapter will seek to provide a deeper understanding of Holy Hip-Hop as a ministry within the broader culture of hip-hop.

MY LOVE FOR HOLY HIP-HOP

I've been listening to Holy Hip-Hop ever since I became a Christian in my teens. After I became a Christian, it was refreshing to find out that I didn't have to abandon my love for hip-hop. I could continue my life as a "hip-hop head" and give glory to the One who brings life! I was able to connect to Gospel Skate Nights, put on by local urban churches, featuring Christian rap.

As noted earlier in the book, when I first stepped into youth ministry I collaborated with other ministries to put on a monthly event called Friday Night Live. It came out of the vision of Elwood Jones, currently the head of Urban Street Level Ministries in the Washington, D.C., area. This monthly Holy Hip-Hop event became a means for many suburban and urban youth to come to Christ. One of the main reasons was that it gave young people themselves opportunities to lead up front. Holy Hip-Hop in my experience allowed gifted young people to rethink how to creatively use their gifts, to be part of leading the church, not just leading *in* the church. Through Holy Hip-Hop, youth can minister within the church walls to create a truly intergenerational church, and they can also be evangelists outside of the church reaching their peers.

As a teen, I used Holy Hip-Hop cassette tapes (I know, I'm giving away my age here) to reach my friends who wouldn't come to church. As young people who have grown up in hip-hop and in the church have become adults, we've seen a rise in Holy Hip-Hop ministries that otherwise would have not been created.

Before I say more about Holy Hip-Hop ministry models that can be developed in the church, let's look at the history and influence of Holy Hip-Hop as its own movement as well as a subculture of hip-hop culture.

THE INFLUENCE OF HOLY HIP-HOP

Does Christian rap or, on a larger scale, Holy Hip-Hop have a significant influence among Christian youth, especially in urban contexts? The reason I emphasize urban youth is that right now the influence of hip-hop culture begins in the city, moves to the suburbs and rural areas, and then goes global. So has Holy Hip-Hop shared a similar history and influence? Let me take you to my answer right off the bat: it is no. I really wish that I could say different, but in my estimation Christian rap doesn't carry as much influence among urban youth as it could. I don't blame Christian rap artists for this. I blame the urban church itself, because except for a few exceptions, rap music and hip-hop culture, whether sacred or secular, is not embraced by the urban church at the level that it could be and in my opinion should be.

I recently spoke at an urban youth conference outside Chicago that was attended mostly by African American churched youth. In a workshop on hip-hop and the church, I asked the young people how many of them were into hip-hop. They all raised their hands. When I followed up with a question about how many listened to Christian rap, only a few raised their hands. Some said they didn't listen to Christian rap because the music was cheesy and many groups seemed gimmicky attempts at being the Christian version of a mainstream group or artist. Some said they thought Christian rap was too judgmental and sounded like some preachers they are forced to listen to on Sunday morning who truly don't understand young people.

As I posed more questions, though, I learned that these young people really didn't know what Holy Hip-Hop is. When I began to mention the names of popular Holy Hip-Hop artists and groups, most of the young people in that room had never heard of them! This means that their opinions about Holy Hip-Hop were being formed without much knowledge of the history or current state of Holy Hip-Hop.

I found this so interesting when I began to connect it with other experiences I have had in leading workshops and discussions about hip-hop. In suburban, mostly European American settings, I have brought up Holy Hip-Hop by using the term "Christian rap," and I have received a strong response from youth and youth workers; they have proved knowledgeable about the artists and even the history. So in my experience at least, some suburban churches know more than urban churches about Holy Hip-Hop. And these young people seem more passionate about it.

When I have talked with parents and other adults in urban churches, sometimes they can't see hip-hop culture beyond the part that glorifies drug use, crime and the degrading of women. Their lack of knowledge of the existence and history of Holy Hip-Hop may reflect the fact that youth in their church share the feelings of those from Chicago that I talked to.

This of course does not speak to all African American urban churches. In fact, in this book we highlight Holy Hip-Hop models within African American urban churches. Further, of course, both Phil Jackson and I are African American urban pastors. Let's look at the history of Holy Hip-Hop, though, to make more sense of the situation.

SOME HOLY HIP-HOP HISTORY

As we look at the history of Christian rap, we'll consider the inability to create a legitimate Holy Hip-Hop culture on a large scale and how this has often prevented the use of hip-hop as a tool for evangelism and outreach. We will, however, look at some examples of how hip-hop *is* being used for evangelism and outreach to urban youth, and I will argue that this should be done by more churches across North America. Even though Holy Hip-Hop has not generated a culture on as large a scale as its so-called secular counterpart, I believe there is a remnant of ministries around the country that won't be denied. I will mention them and explore the models they provide. I will also provide a biblical foundation for my argument for a Holy Hip-Hop movement resourced and supported by the African American urban church.

My first experience with Christian rap was through a church in south Minneapolis, Park Avenue United Methodist Church. Back in the 1970s and 1980s, Park Avenue would put on an annual eight-day music festival, the Soul Liberation Festival, right in the heart of the city. I wonder if this festival featuring a diversity of urban and gospel music was the first of its kind. I was about to become a senior in high school in the summer of 1987 when I first experienced Christian rap at this event. Through the Soul Liberation Festival I was introduced to groups like the Lumpkins Family, ETW (End Time Warriors), and Preachers in Disguise (which at the time featured my now good friend Fred Lynch) and the solo artist Michael Peace. This was the first time I had heard rap about Jesus Christ. I would consider myself a true hip-hop head, having grown up to the sounds of Soul Sonic Force, Run-DMC, Kurtis Blow and Whodini, but I had never heard of any of the rap groups at Soul Lib before. I had just recently become a Christian and had gone through a phase of thinking I could no longer listen to "secular" music, so I had thrown out all of my hip-hop music. No longer were Run-DMC and Whodini in my music collection. They had been replaced by Commissioned, the Winans, Carmen and Take Six. As hard as it was, I was willing to give up hip-hop in order to follow Jesus. As a matter of fact, the reason I had come to the Soul Liberation Festival that year was to hear Commissioned and the Winans. I had no idea that I would be introduced to Christian rap!

I learned more about Christian rap as I connected with other young people in the youth group at Park Avenue. Through a friend named Joey in the group, I learned that DC Talk was actually one of the first rap groups to record and get major distribution within the Christian music market. In the car of a youth minister named Steve Floyd, Joey put in a cassette of DC Talk as we rode to a conference in Milwaukee (Julian Montgomery, later the founder of TKM Records, was there as well; we were all teens at the time). Being made up of two European American guys and one African American guy, this group, in my opinion, had a sound that didn't compare in quality to the rap I was used to listening to. To be honest, I thought their rhymes were kind of cheesy. The content of the rap was different. I was used to lyrics about what was going on in the hood, whether from a social consciousness standpoint or a party perspective. I wasn't used to a group that was predominantly white with "cheesy" lyrics. Well, eventually DC Talk got out of the rap game (seems the black guy in the group, Michael Tait, didn't like rap much anyway), but since then another member, who today goes by the name Toby Mac, has not only used elements of hip-hop culture in his music but also started a record label called Gotee Records with some partners, and it features current rap groups such as G.R.I.T.S. and L.A. Symphony.

Meanwhile I dove deep into the world of Christian rap, connecting with groups such as I.D.O.L. King, Freedom of Soul, Soldiers for Christ, Transformation Crusade, D.O.C. (Disciples of Christ) and A-1 Swift. I also was introduced to solo artists such as D-Boy Rodriguez (who was killed before we could truly experience his greatness), Mike-E, Steven Wiley and Lady J. There was a Christian book and record store in my neighborhood at the time, and a radio deejay named Lonnie Lowe educated me on Christian rap artists. Some of these groups, like I.D.O.L. King, had the flow and sound to hold their own with so-called secular groups, but others just couldn't. Many of the groups and solo artists did have talent, but typically they didn't have the financial backing to compete in production and distribution.

Most Christian rap artists I know did grow up in the inner city. Since that's the case, why do the many urban youth I've talked to feel they can't relate to Christian rap and that much of Christian rap doesn't relate to them?

For reasons fair or unfair, Christian rap has had to fight a reputation of not being at the same level as so-called secular rap. Many people have assumed over the years that Christian rap was mainly for those who weren't gifted enough to do "real" hip-hop. I have to admit that sometimes this stereotype corresponds to reality. I've heard Christian rap that seems to reflect the notion that all you need is to love Jesus and have a microphone and a beat machine, and you can be a professional Christian rapper. You're not going to be very influential, though, when you're seen as the farm league of hip-hop, and Christian rap has had to battle this perception.

End Time Warriors, a Christian hip-hop group in the early '90s

End Time Warriors and DC Talk

Photos courtesy of Forbes Designs.

Grape Tree Records, for example, released way too many artists on their label in the 1990s. They seemed so committed to being the number-one seller of Christian rap (which at the time wasn't a very lofty goal) that they couldn't focus on the production, distribution and marketing of just a few high-quality artists who could have made them a serious force in hip-hop as a whole. A few Grape Tree artists were really good, but the obsession with being the largest Holy Hip-Hop label resulted in loading down Christian bookstore shelves with a lot of Holy Hip-Hop projects that lacked quality production. Still today there are some Christian rap CDs on shelves of Christian book and record stores that shouldn't be there, because of record labels and distribution channels run by Euro-American Christians who just don't have the connections or history to distinguish between quality Holy Hip-Hop and a work in progress.

To be fair, Grape Tree Records was working with the limited resources that were available at the time. I believe that if churches around the country with a heart for reaching unchurched youth had put adequate resources behind Grape Tree, the production would have been stronger and many artists on the label might still be around today. I praise God for Grape Tree Records' serving as a pioneer within Holy Hip-Hop with what they had. I also praise God for predominantly European American record labels and distribution centers out of Nashville that, despite their limited knowledge of hip-hop, believed it was important to put out rap artists who glorify God.

Nevertheless, Holy Hip-Hop has roots in national distribution sources and not the inner city of New York, and for this reason it has faced challenges in reaching unchurched hip-hoppers at the level I believe it could. The facts that DC Talk was seen as the roots of Christian rap and that early groups and artists were recorded and distributed by "white" Christian organizations hindered the influence of Christian rap from the onset. Fred Lynch, who began in a group known as Preacher in Disguise in the 1980s, has told me stories about concert tours of that group in connection with Josh McDowell Ministries. How can you be seen as having origins in and connections to urban youth culture and the urban church if the main shows that you minister in are more connected to the predominantly white Bible Belt?

Keep in mind that "secular" rap music began in the urban grassroots setting of the Bronx in the 1970s, generated by urban youth and young adults who were mostly African American and Latino. It's much easier to be influenced by something you feel your people created. Influence is also much more natural if what was birthed is more than just music, if it includes fashion, language, street knowledge—an entire urban subculture.

Unfortunately, Christian rap has roots more in predominantly white Christian conferences, festivals and other events than in urban areas. Even today Christian rap groups and artists can be heard more often at predominantly white Christian youth events, conferences, youth worker conventions and festivals out in the woods than in big cities. Even the African American-led megachurches that bring Christian rap artists and groups in for youth conferences and events are in many cases located outside the inner-city community.

ACCESS TO HOLY HIP-HOP

Could you imagine the impact of Holy Hip-Hop if it put down new roots in local urban churches that would use hip-hop proactively to reach a generation that is growing up in hip-hip (in contrast to their parents and grandparents, who grew up in the church)? Could you imagine the impact if as so-called secular hip-hop came off the inner-city streets, Holy Hip-Hop came out of the sanctuary of the urban church? The local church ought to be the birthing place of Holy Hip-Hop artists. The Sunday morning worship experience, youth ministry and evangelistic outreaches are all places where Holy Hip-Hop artists with shown talent ought to develop their craft. The local church should not only provide the opportunity for these emerging artists and ministers but should also launch them out into the broader hip-hop culture in order to advance Christianity among their unchurched peers. It ain't happening yet: I haven't found evidence on a large scale of African American urban churches engaging hip-hop culture as a whole or embracing and supporting Holy Hip-Hop. Could it be that white suburban churched youth know more about Christian rap than urban youth? How many urban youth really know about Cross Movement or G.R.I.T.S.? How would they, if no church in their neighborhood has targeted them and has decided to use Holy Hip-Hop as a tool to reach them? Which audience are Christian rap artists really trying to reach through their ministry? Trust me, if they say they want to reach all youth I will say amen, but I have a feeling their opportunities to reach and influence inner-city youth with a Holy Hip-Hop gospel are minimal compared to the opportunities to minister in front of predominantly white crowds.

An important reason that Christian rap has a hard time becoming more influential among urban youth has to do with how you get to it. Until recently, for the most part you could get Christian rap only by going to Christian bookstores, which tend to be in the suburbs and in my opinion are church friendly but not very youth friendly—and not urban youth friendly at all. I just have no reason to think that urban youth will run to Christian bookstores in droves to get Christian rap. Another problem is that for the most part Christian radio is dominated by traditional and contemporary "white" Christian music. Urban "secular" radio stations that are playing rap aren't playing G.R.I.T.S., Cross Movement or John Reuben. The Cross Movement writes in their song "When I Flow," off the *Holy Culture* CD: "Where the buzz? / Better yet, where's the love? / Seems like, what we got wrecks the clubs. / There's no hugs, probably cause there's no drugs. / And no mansion that's housing thugs."

So how then does Christian rap get into the ears and hands of urban youth? African American-led urban churches need to embrace Holy Hip-Hop, because by using hip-hop as an outreach and discipleship tool these churches can get the music into the ears of urban youth. The reason urban youth hear the type of rap that they do hear is that there are institutions making sure it gets to them. Can we blame urban youth totally for what they listen to if we, the institution known as the church, aren't trying to get an alternative to them?

WHAT THE CHURCH CAN DO ABOUT HOLY HIP-HOP

There is much that the church can do to support Holy Hip-Hop and use to reach those living in hip-hop culture and outside the church. For one, churches could put on a monthly hip-hop service and either bring in national Holy Hip-Hop groups or give local youth who are gifted in the elements of hip-hop the opportunity to reach their peers.

Throw a Holy Hip-Hop dance party at church where young people can invite friends who wouldn't normally come to church. This can be a social alternative for young people on a Friday or Saturday night, free of the negative pressures of other parties that may be going on.

You could start a Holy Hip-Hop record store in your church. As noted earlier, one of the issues with Holy Hip-Hop is how it gets to young people. The church must be the vehicle to get Christian rap into the ears of this generation.

Why not treat Holy Hip-Hop artists as missionaries to this generation and to hip-hop culture? If you are a youth minister, play Holy Hip-Hop every time you get the chance—in the van, on the bus, in the youth room. If you have a room in the church building dedicated to youth, put up posters of Holy Hip-Hop groups; this way your young people will get more familiar with these artists.

When you talk about Holy Hip-Hop groups, call them "underground groups" within hip-hop instead of Christian rap groups; this is especially important if the young people you're talking to don't identify themselves as Christian.

I have found when I contact Holy Hip-Hop record labels and distribution companies directly and share my heart to bring Holy Hip-Hop to this generation, they are very helpful and often send me free stuff. The urban church, as well as churches outside the city full of "hip-hop heads," ought to be a grassroots warehouse of Holy Hip-Hop.

SHOULD WE USE THE TERM "HOLY HIP-HOP"?

Some within Holy Hip-Hop are not sure that "Christian rap" and "Holy Hip-Hop" are terms that should be used by Christian artists who are trying to influence urban youth. The rap group Anointed Kings Alliance, who are members of the church where I pastor in Minneapolis, and I have had this very discussion. I talked more in depth with one of the members, Damon Washington, also known as D-Dub. He feels that being labeled a Holy Hip-Hop artist actually limits the calling he has to serve as a minister within hip-hop culture as a whole. The question discussed earlier came up in our discussion: Could it be that the marketing of rap artists and groups by predominantly white (and even traditional black gospel) record companies has actually isolated them from the very young people they most want to reach? Further, are they being forced, consciously or unconsciously, to write lyrics that mostly focus on an individualistic approach to salvation, versus a more holistic approach that could encompass the societal and institutional issues that some aspects of "secular" rap deals with?

If Christian rap is geared to mainly reach an already churched audience, it is missing out on a greater influence that could be explored among urban unchurched youth. It comes down to whether Holy Hip-Hop is to be primarily used to reach out to unchurched youth or to disciple and provide a hip-hop alternative to already Christian youth. My hope is that the movement would be large enough and holistic enough to do both. If the church, especially the larger congregations, put financial resources into Holy Hip-Hop as an outreach tool, Christian rap artists could be marketed to an unchurched audience as simply hip-hop artists, not Holy Hip-Hop artists. For connecting with churches that are unfamiliar with Holy Hip-Hop though, it's important to use the term "Holy Hip-Hop" in order to educate these churches that such music that is relevant to the culture and gives glory to God does exist. This is important especially in the African American context, because there is a tradition of God being a centerpiece of the culture. God and the church were key to our coming out of slavery and to the advancement of the civil rights movement, and now they can be be a major influence in hip-hop culture.

So I don't believe there is a need to abandon the term "Holy Hip-Hop" or "Christian." But when I'm connecting with a non-Christian, the first words out of my mouth are not that I'm an African American urban Christian. I start off talking about things we have in common already. I'm trying to build a relationship with them, make a connection that will give me opportunities to proclaim Christ in a way that will be heard. Similarly, Holy Hip-Hop artists should be presented to the unchurched in ways that create an opportunity to be heard. In the end it comes down to who the Holy Hip-Hop artist's target audience is.

HOLY HIP-HOP MINISTRY MODELS

A number of existing ministries do use elements of hip-hop culture in their discipleship, outreach and worship. Crossover Community Church began as the first hip-hop church in January 2000 in Tampa, Florida. It's led by hip-hop artist Urban Disciple, known by his congregation as Pastor Tommy Kyllonen. This is truly a hip-hop church, featuring hip-hop praise and worship over tracks played by a deejay. When I visited this ministry, I was deeply moved by the impact it is having in the community. Beautiful graffiti art can be found both inside and outside the building. There is an outside skate park. Annually the church puts on a national hip-hop conference and festival where attendees can not only explore their unique approach to hip-hop church but also hear from pastors and artists from other hip-hop ministries. My hope is that what he is truly doing is pioneering a work which points us to the emerging multiethnic and urban church. I pray for the day that we see multiple hip-hop churches around the country engaging culture and creating culture in order to build God's kingdom. For more information on this church, hip-hop resources and the annual conference on hip-hop ministry, go to <www.crossoverchurch.org>.

Craig and Zola Allen, youth directors at New Life Fellowship in Elmhurst-Queens, New York, use hip-hop for outreach and discipleship. Through the Beats and Blessings Academy they have developed an after-school program in the church where youth can develop their own demo project. Through this program they've been able to reach out to and raise up a multicultural army of young people; some of them even lead worship on Sunday morning. Through this ministry, youth in New York's hip-hop community are learning how to use and further develop their gifts and passions. The outcome is youth who are involved in the church in a significant way and are creating projects to reach their peers who aren't in the church.

At the 2003 Youth for Christ national event DC/LA, Holy Hip-Hop pioneer Fred Lynch premiered his Gospel of John in hip-hop form (quoted at the beginning of the chapter) to over twenty thousand youth in three cities. He continues to promote this project at conferences and youth events, with the goal of completing both the Old and New Testaments in hip-hop style! In the appendix you'll find the web address that you can use to order his Gospel of John.

Cross Movement Ministries has grown from a rap group from Philadelphia to a ministry committed to growing a holy culture. This group has been part of the Impact Movement, launched out of Campus Crusade for Christ as a ministry committed to equipping African American Christian leaders. Cross Movement has brought not only Holy Hip-Hop to the emerging generation but a relevant theology as well, for its members are not only quality artists but also deep theological thinkers. I've heard one of the members of the group, Ambassador or "Deuce," bring the Word in a powerful way. He is a seminary-trained hip-hop artist and preacher. This can only advance the bridging of the church and hip-hop.

Gotee Records has become more than just a major player as a Christian record label; it is creating culture through its term "Hip-Hope," which is the title of a multiple-volume compilation project. Using the term "Hip-Hope" rather than "Holy Hip-Hop" probably will allow its artists to reach deeper into the larger hip-hop culture.

There is my partner in writing this book, Phil Jackson, serving as pastor of The House, the first youth and young adult hip-hop church of Chicago. Later in this book Phil will provide in-depth information about this distinctive church.

In my own home church, the Anointed Kings Alliance (A.K.A.), under the umbrella of our Sanctuary Community Development Corporation, has started the Hip-Hop Academy. This is an after-school outreach program held in both a local elementary and a high school in north Minneapolis. It focuses on teaching young people the true elements and roots of hip-hop culture as a whole and ends with a community performance in the school auditorium where the young people themselves break dance, rap, deejay and share poetry. The Hip-Hop Academy allows our church opportunities to connect with youth and families in our neighborhood and to influence their lives through activities that are relevant to their daily life. It explores both "secular" and Christian expressions of hip-hop culture and focuses on developing stronger critical thinking skills within youth to help them make future choices on what music they will buy and listen to. The program also gives Anointed Kings Alliance an opportunity to share their Christian expression of hip-hop culture. A.K.A. also has a CD out whose lyrics can help already Christian youth move to a deeper place in their walk with God. Thus A.K.A. has the capacity to use Holy Hip-Hop for both outreach to unchurched youth and discipleship of Christian youth. A.K.A.'s community-based outreach works in part because of the support of a local church that is committed to engaging those living in hip-hop culture and outside the church.

Through TKM Records, Julian Montgomery, who is also part of my congregation, has released not only his solo project *Fruit of the Spirit* but allowed me to make my debut as an artist through the compilation *Soul Cutz* Volume 1. Julian sought out artists in various local churches for this compilation, which not only has given them a chance to use their gifts but also has helped to connect their home churches to hip-hop culture where that connection was not already made. The church ought to be an alternative place to discover, develop and showcase hip-hop artists.

I have to mention Elwood and Betty Jones, the founders of Urban Street Level Ministries, combining go-go, neo-soul and hip-hop to present the tightest urban contemporary praise and worship I have ever heard in my life! Not only are Betty and Elwood pioneers of this type of praise and worship, but they were the first to put on a Midwest Holy Hip-Hop festival when they created Hood-Fest years ago. This festival went on for three years on the north side of Minneapolis. It ended after that, in part, because Elwood and Betty moved out East. Still today, from their home base of Washington, D.C., they provide seminars and workshops and are a featured worship band at many conferences and events (you can find out more at 301-332-1807).

There are many other artists, groups and ministries using hip-hop to create a holy culture. At the end of the book there is a resource section that lists as many of them as we could find, but keep in mind that this is in no way an exhaustive list. I hope the examples here inspire you regarding the great impact the church can have by using elements of hip-hop culture to reach those influenced by it. Ministries like these truly will use hip-hop to influence urban youth with the good news of Jesus Christ. These emerging hip-hop leaders are shaping the future of the urban church—a church that is multiethnic, postblack and postwhite, and engaging hip-hop culture in creative ways.

I believe we need a Holy Hip-Hop movement that is larger than record labels and hip-hop awards. We need a movement that will plant churches and parachurch ministries, develop a practical theology, raise up a new generation of preachers and leaders, and spread to college campuses and seminaries around the United States and wherever hip-hop has become part of the culture.

AN OPPORTUNITY FOR THE CHURCH

The church ought to be engaging hip-hop culture but should be seeking to create Holy Hip-Hop culture as well. Christian artists should not settle for being the Christian version of a "secular" movement; the church should *birth* movements. Beginning with the civil rights movement, the African American church has a history of engaging the surrounding culture in order to be used by God to bring change and transformation. The Cross Movement's title track of their *Holy Culture* CD (2003) is a wake-up call to the church: "All we do is pray, stay, build, chill, walk the, talk the, spark the Holy Culture! / Live, give, speak with meekness . . . / Week out and week in, spark the Holy Culture!" We can be a creative and transforming cultural force in the world.

We are called to all nations to make disciples: "And Jesus came up and spoke to them, saying, 'All authority has been given to Me in heaven and on earth. Go therefore and make disciples of all the nations'" (Matthew 28:18-19). Nations are made up of generations, cultures and subcultures, and we must speak into them all to carry out the mission given to us by the Lord. How will we go into the hip-hop culture and make disciples? This is the question for the church today. Our God who has all authority will empower us to reach this culture for his kingdom. The same God who empowers us is the Creator of the universe, and this creation power should lead us to create a Holy Hip-Hop culture through the church.

John 1:3 tells us, "All things came into being through Him, and apart from Him nothing came into being that has come into being." I believe that at least some aspects of hip-hop culture can be attributed to Christ. Of course not all of hip-hop culture should be attributed to him, but could original purposes such as love and peace be attributed to him? Could original elements such as dance and rap be attributed to him? Hip-hop at some level can be used as a ministry tool. We can embrace a Holy Hip-Hop culture, or at least, as Cross Movement says, call the hip-hop community to become a holy culture. In either case there must be an engagement of hip-hop that doesn't just treat hip-hop as an enemy. Ambassador writes in "Thesis Pieces" off *The Thesis* CD: "On one side we wanna represent Christ to the culture. / Hip-hop mostly knows him for making tight little posters. / Or a sculpture, but they can't view Him like they're supposed to. / Cause the gospel's never been preached to them like it's supposed to."

Genesis tells us: "God created the great sea monsters and every living creature that moves, with which the waters swarmed after their kind, and every winged bird after its kind; and God saw that it was good. . . . Then God said, 'Let Us make man in Our image, according to Our likeness'" (1:21, 26). God is creative, and we are made in his image. Shouldn't we be creative in the culture that we live in? In order to fulfill the Great Commission, shouldn't we create a Holy Hip-Hop culture that stands on its own and doesn't simply borrow ideas and beats from "secular" hip-hop?

There was a time when the best "soul" music came out of the church. The best rhythm and blues artists had their beginning in the African American church. It seemed in the period of soul music that having been involved in the church in some way was a prerequisite for becoming a professional singer. When I was an interim pastor at Redeemer Missionary Baptist Church in the mid-1990s, soul singer Ann Nesby, who started out with the gospel group Sounds of Blackness and then went on as a solo artist recording with soul singers such as Al Green, would visit our church. When she was there, our minister of music, Tim Veasy, would always have her sing a solo or join the choir. Many soul singers have a connection to the church, and when they go on to become "secular" artists, they find a way to stay connected to the church. Superstar singer Stevie Wonder has stayed connected to West Angeles Church of God in Christ. An issue of *Ebony* magazine focusing on the new "black spirituality" carried a photo of soul/hip-hop singer Usher attending New Birth Church in Atlanta.

Because hip-hop culture, in contrast, was created outside the church, having roots in the streets became the prerequisite for rising up in the movement, for the most part. In order for a true Holy Hip-Hop movement to develop, then, we need a new model of hip-hop artists and theologians who are raised up in the urban church. With intentionality on the part of the local church, a Holy Hip-Hop culture can be created that should carry an anointing and power that "secular" hip-hop does not. What if through this movement the church was able to produce hip-hop artists marked by an excellence beyond that of the mainstream hip-hop movement? It is possible to create an alternative culture while living in a larger culture. The book of Daniel provides a model. At the time Jerusalem had been taken over by Babylon, and the king of Babylon, Nebuchadnezzar, ordered that certain youth be taken and trained in various aspects of the culture, such as language and diet. Daniel was one of them. Daniel decided to not eat the same foods that the other youth were being trained to eat. He created a way to live in the culture but have a distinctive diet—and he and others on the diet proved to be healthier than others in the culture. Just so, Holy Hip-Hop is about artists and ministers that live in the culture but have a different "diet," choices that lead to a healthier outcome. There are ministries all around the country that model this movement of hip-hop, and the outcome of their alternative culture is transformed lives.

If after reading all of this you sense a call to develop your own hip-hop ministry but don't know where to begin, have no fear: Sound Changers Ministry is here. This ministry, led by three anointed women, Kim Neptune, Cheryl Rouse and Channon Lemon, is a national resource developed with the vision to equip the church to reach urban youth and young adults living in hip-hop culture. It offers a magazine featuring articles on how to develop a hip-hop service; a broad listing of hip-hop ministries; and book resources. Sound Changers' goal is to come alongside the African American church in order to reclaim a generation in hip-hop. (It is located in Cary, North Carolina, telephone 919-859-3188.)

I believe your church and ministry can make this kind of impact.

Take time to pray and think through the ways your church is positioned to reach the emerging generation and use elements of hip-hop to design new ministry models. Put on an annual Holy Hip-Hop festival of your own. Set aside some space in your church building to create your own Christian rap store. Bring in a hip-hop artist and theologian to speak to parents and youth about what is going on in hip-hop culture and how to bring the message of Jesus into it. If your resources are low, partner with other churches and organize a citywide event! Look for up-and-coming Holy Hip-Hop artists within your own church and encourage them in their gifts. Go get *The Epic* hip-hop Gospel of John and use it as a Bible study in your youth ministry. These are just a few ideas to get you started, and I trust God to give you more as you venture into building a hip-hop church of your own.

7

THE Emcee AND THE PREACHER

The Connection Between Rap and the Black Preaching Tradition

In his song "Hip-Hop It Don't Stop" off *The Fruit of the Spirit* CD, Julian writes: "Recognize hip-hop is here to stay / If you don't you'll just have to get out tha way . . . / Wit kicks thumpin', speakers bumpin' and people yellin' Ho . . . / I know you can't understand everything said, / But ain't that the same case when you holler from the pulpit? / Hip-hop's the new tool used to reach the streets. / I'm just trying to educate you wit this abstract beat." If we want our preaching to be heard, then we need to learn a few lessons from the emcee.

THE INFLUENCE OF THE EMCEE

The emcee is the most influential of the four foundational elements of hip-hop, even though it's the youngest. Whether you are a hip-hop head or not, you are probably aware of names of rappers such as Eminem, Will Smith, Snoop Dog, Jay-Z and the legendary Notorious B.I.G. and Tupac. And even for the serious hip-hop head, it probably is much harder to name deejays, break dancers and graffiti artists. At a youth conference where I was presenting a workshop on hip-hop, the youth present were able to

name many emcees, some deejays, but no break dancers or graffiti artists. In hip-hop the one who holds the microphone has the
power of ultimate influence.

As I grew up in hip-hop, I was initially educated on it through
the voice of hip-hop, the emcee. Through the emcee you learn the
history, culture, philosophies and doctrines of hip-hop. The quality
of hip-hop in the ears of the listener is based on the ability and
flow of the emcee. There is no hooking of a generation into the
culture of hip-hop without the emcee.

The emcee initially came on the scene as a partner to the deejay, to assist in rocking the party right. It seems to me that in the
beginning of hip-hop the deejay was Batman and the emcee was
Robin, but the script was flipped as hip-hop went mainstream in
the late 1980s, so that the emcee is now Batman. Chuck D, the
lead emcee of Public Enemy, says that hip-hop is "the Black
CNN," and if we stick with that analogy, the emcee is the lead
evening anchor.

You can learn a lot about various ethnic and urban street cultures through the emcee. He or she must be knowledgeable of urban street language, style and culture in order to earn the right to
be listened to. Hip-hop listeners want to know what's really going
on in the street. They want to know who's keeping it real. They
want to know what the cool fashion styles are and what the cool
places to hang out are, and the emcee must be educated enough
to let the listener know this and more. The emcee is telling the listener what's really going on from their perspective, and they are
presenting a way of living within urban culture. The emcee is also
reporting to you how they feel about institutions and organizations
that influence urban culture—the government, the police and
even the church.

This doesn't mean I think emcees are right in all that they say
as they spit lyrics on all of these things; I'm just laying out the

scope of their vocal influence. The emcee can choose to use their gifts and knowledge in a way that educates and uplifts the listener or degrades and downgrades the listener. This is why, though the emcee is the most influential element within hip-hop, it's also the most controversial. If the listener is unaware of the context and motives of the emcee as they spit out their lyrics, the emcee can be the most misunderstood of all the elements of hip-hop as well.

Though the emcee is the vocal centerpiece of an entire culture, neither one emcee alone nor five emcees in a group can reflect all of hip-hop culture. Since hip-hop *is* a culture, it includes good and bad, beautiful and ugly. We have to be aware that there are good lyrics and bad lyrics, beautiful lyrics and ugly lyrics, uplifting lyrics and degrading lyrics. All of this is hip-hop, and we should not be worshipers of emcees, nor should we be bashers of all emcees.

THE POWER OF THE EMCEE

Many who love or hate hip-hop do so primarily based on what they hear in the rap of the emcee. For many listeners, the emcee can make or break hip-hop. If you turn on your television and see a rap video, usually a particular emcee is presented. The emcee is center stage, using bleeped-out vulgar language, and the lyrical content that remains is very sexual in nature. Women with not much clothing on dance around a male with lots of jewelry on. This alone can cause a Christian to reject hip-hop culture altogether. I have heard many pastors bash hip-hop because they are familiar only with rappers who spit degrading and harmful lyrics. I myself have serious problems with this aspect of hip-hop culture. You tend to see this style more often in the form known as gangsta rap. Hip-hop intellectual Michael Eric Dyson has an interesting take on even this form of hip-hop:

> Despite its many problems, however, gangsta rap is not the most pressing problem that black folks face. The material

suffering of the ghetto poor, the predicament of young black teens, the conservative onslaught against black interest and culture, and the devastating consequences of drug economies, for instance, are far more urgent. That is not to deny that gangsta rap's repulsive misogyny, virulent homophobia, and verbal violence are not cause for concern. They are. But the vilification that gangsta rap has endured, and its mostly young black male artists right along with it, is far out of proportion to the problems it presents. The demonization of gangsta rappers is often a convenient excuse for cultural and political elites to pounce on a group of artists who are easy prey. The much more difficult task is to find out what conditions cause their anger and hostility.

(PREFACE TO *BETWEEN GOD AND GANGSTA RAP*, P. XIII)

If a church has decided to engage hip-hop culture and the emcees within it, it would do well to consider Dyson's comments. Dyson calls us to wrestle with what produces gangsta rappers and their lyrics. Did they just come up with those disturbing images on their own, or does the environment in which they grew up and those who have abandoned them play a role? We must not wrestle just with Dyson's challenge, though; we must also wrestle with why many record companies and music video television stations seemed to be obsessed with the gangsta emcee.

TYPES OF EMCEES

There are other emcees such as Holy Hip-Hop emcees, social consciousness emcees and showman emcees.

Holy Hip-Hop emcees are Christian theologians using rap lyrics to present the gospel of Jesus Christ to those living in hip-hop culture and outside the church. I broke this down in the chapter on Holy Hip-Hop, so I won't spend a lot of time here. The problem is the Holy Hip-Hop emcees aren't given the kind of platform that other types of emcees are given in our society. You're mainly going to hear and see this type of emcee on cable television Christian stations such as the Trinity Broadcasting Network, the Word Network or Sunday mornings on Black Entertainment Television. Holy Hip-Hop emcees such as Cross Movement and G.R.I.T.S. have gotten airplay only rarely on more mainstream and prime-time rap shows on cable. The best place to catch these emcees is at a live event.

Social consciousness emcees not only educate the listener on what's going on in urban culture but also provides some knowledge on how to improve one's life. The social consciousness emcee wants to change the conditions of the inner city. This emcee speaks out against injustice and points us back to the original principles of hip-hop culture of peace, unity and community. The social consciousness emcee wants to enlighten the listener on culture, history and/or religion. Common, Mos Def and KRS-ONE are examples of this type of emcee.

The showman emcee is the Bill Cosby of rappers. These emcees just want to entertain the crowd, and they position themselves as appropriate for the whole family. Emcees such as Will Smith, M.C. Hammer, Biz Markie and L.L. Cool J. are a few I would put in this category. These emcees want the listener to have fun, which is another one of the original principles of hip-hop culture. They don't feel the need to use explicit language in order to get the listener connected to hip-hop.

All of these types of emcees have made rap music powerful through diversity, and this is why there is a global hip-hop influence, connecting listeners based on their tastes.

So though the emcee is not the only element of hip-hop, in my opinion it is the primary element. Some in hip-hop will disagree with me, especially if they are not an emcee or if they have gifts in other elements. But since I'm not an emcee myself, I hope I'm giving something of an unbiased perspective. But what is the connection between the emcee/rapper and the black preaching style and tradition?

THE BLACK PREACHING TRADITION

I focus on the black preaching tradition in relation to rapping for a couple of reasons. First, the black preaching tradition, like rapping, has historically spoken into social movements and struggles. Black preaching began in the context of slavery, questioning the slave owner's Christianity. Then it moved to comparing the Christianity of the slave owner with the Christianity that began in northern Africa. Black preaching is about freedom! The black preaching tradition moved next to address Jim Crow segregation and prophetically developed and moved us through the civil rights movement. Black preaching today continues to look at the social issues of our time, commenting on such issues as the war in Iraq, abortion, marriage, hip-hop culture and even the Michael Jackson case. Maybe "Black CNN" reporting didn't begin in hip-hop but in the black church!

Second, black preaching includes rhythm and song; it's the originator of the "whoop." Though not accompanied by a deejay, it is supported by the organ and the drums. The black preaching tradition includes call and response, where the preaching feeds off the "talk back" of the congregation as people call out "Amen" and "Go ahead and preach!" Black preaching is full of emotion and passion. It demands a response from the listeners, not only through the call and response but also through a commitment to action. Black preaching has led to marches, boycotts and sit-ins.

TYPES OF BLACK PREACHERS

There are various types of black preachers as well: whooping preachers, storytelling preachers, prosperity preachers, social justice preachers and holiness preachers. Some black preachers are a mix of a couple of types, and maybe the same could be said of emcees as well. The *African American Pulpit* is a quarterly journal put out by Judson Press and coedited by Martha Simmons and Frank Thomas, which tells the history as well as explores the present state of the art of black preaching.

Just as I grew up listening to emcees such as Slick Rick, Rakim, Eric Sermon (now that name makes a connection) and Kool Mo Dee, I also grew up listening to black preachers such as Martin Luther King Jr., Gardner Taylor, E. V. Hill, Tom Skinner, Tony Evans, Buster Sories and Jesse Jackson. I said earlier if you want to know what's going on in hip-hop you have to pay attention to the emcee; well, if you want to know what's going on in the black church, you have to pay attention to the black preacher!

Like hip-hop culture, the black church culture is marked by distinct elements. I use the term *culture* because in some ways the black church is very similar to the Christian church at large, but in many other ways it's unique. The elements are similar, but the way those elements are expressed is unique because it is based in culture. You can't talk about the black church and not talk about black culture, because the black church came out of a fight for freedom, liberation, justice and the search for an intimate relationship with God for African Americans in the midst of slavery, segregation and other manifestations of racism.

"The key to understanding the different styles of preaching is in the word culture: Preaching is carried out in the idiom, imagery, style, and world view of a particular people" (Henry H. Mitchell, *Black Preaching*, p. 11). When I think of the black church, many things come to mind—gospel music, soul food, social justice. But all of that also points me to in some way to the black preacher. The black preacher is the key component of the black church. Through the whoop, the black preacher is a musical communicator. The sermon of a preacher in the black preaching tradition is served up as soul food for the soul. The black preacher, as expressed Martin Luther King Jr. said, is a "drum major of justice." The black church begins with the black preacher. And black preaching is rooted in black culture. "Without Black culture, there could be no Black preaching" (Mitchell, *Black Preaching,* p. 12).

Just as rap has pioneers such as the SugarHill Gang, Run-DMC and Kurtis Blow, black preaching had early pioneers such as the Reverends Harry Hoosier, Richard Allen and Lemuel Haynes. What I love about Henry H. Mitchell's book on black preaching is that he presents it as a true cultural art form:

> Black preaching is inherently dependent on call and response. African music and oral communication are characterized by considerable audience participation. The audience is deeply involved in the tale, which is presented in picturesque language and great animation. Even today, congregations of the Black masses feel cheated if no place for their response is provided. Black music is full of this antiphonal element as well.
>
> (*BLACK PREACHING,* P. 31)

Just as black preaching is an art form, so is rapping. Used to glorify God, rapping could be just as effective today with urban youth and young adults as is preaching, if not more so. This is not to say that the days of black preaching are over. I feel black preaching and rapping are both here to stay, though rapping needs more time to prove itself, while the legacy of black preaching seems to be established.

PREACHING AND RAPPING

Let's continue to build bridges between the emcee and the preacher. Bridges can be built when two things that have been separate are revealed to have some common history and values—in the analogy used earlier in this book, some "well" of common ground. When Jesus met the Samaritan woman at the well, he broke down historically developed barriers in order to begin the process of Jews and Samaritans' becoming one in Christ Jesus. A preacher today might well picture himself or herself as a religious Jewish leader and the hip-hop emcee as a modern-day Samaritan. They may find a bridge, or a well, in a common history and some values shared by rap and the black preaching tradition, such as roots in African storytelling.

Could these two art forms from African American culture begin learning from each other? I believe that the church has an opportunity to better preach the gospel message to those outside the church if it will pay closer attention to hip-hop culture through the lyrics of the emcee. Remember, when Chuck D calls rap the Black CNN, he is calling the emcee an urban news reporter of sorts. Emcees speak to the social ills surrounding them within urban culture. In much-loved hip-hop raps such as "The Message" by Grandmasters Flash and Melle Mel this is evident: "Don't push me cause I'm close to the edge, / I'm trying not to lose my head. / It's like a jungle sometimes / it makes me wonder / how I keep from going under."

The social consciousness emcee is especially like the black preacher in this regard. As noted above, this emcee is trying to educate the listener about what is going on in the city and calling for justice. This emcee is not trying to impress the listener but to educate the listener. Presentations in this style of rap can encompass both cultural and spiritual knowledge. (Because hip-hop culture was created outside the church, it's understandable that Christianity is not at the center of the spiritual knowledge that rap usually presents. Keep in mind the context: hip-hop is an expression of African American inner-city culture, and socially conscious rap speaks out against the dominant oppressive culture. Throughout the history of America, Christianity has mostly had a Eurocentric slant, so it's not surprising that groups have arisen to offer a different take on African American spirituality, such as the Nation of Islam and the Five Percent Nation.)

You can't talk about hip-hop without talking about African American youth and African American culture, and this is best expressed through the emcee. Also, you can't talk about the black church without talking about African American culture, and this is best expressed through black preaching. Both hip-hop and the black church have roots in the African American experience. You can talk about neither hip-hop nor the black church without looking at issues of justice, race and the inner city or elements of song, shouting, praising and storytelling.

Both rap and black preaching are marked by various elements and techniques. Both rap and black preaching are rooted in the African storytelling tradition. Both rap and black preaching speak to issues of injustice. Both rap and black preaching have great influence on European Americans as well as people of other ethnicities. When you broaden the discussion to include other elements besides rapping and preaching, you really see the global parallels. Both hip-hop and black gospel music (which comes out of the black church) have heavy influence in places like Australia, England and Japan. Just as there are rap concert tours in Japan, there are gospel choir tours in London.

Let's dig a little deeper. Rhythm and blues is considered to have been birthed by the black church, as soul music greats such as Aretha Franklin and Marvin Gaye were children of black preachers. Then, as Nelson George says, hip-hop has been held responsible for "the death of rhythm and blues." Though rhythm and blues is not totally dead, hip-hop does point us to the fact that we live in a postsoul or post-rhythm and blues culture. Hip-hop does move to actually remix rhythm and blues than to kill it. Some may even say that hip-hop gave rhythm and blues a new life. In the case of Holy Hip-Hop, gospel music even gets new life. Secular rap artists and group such as Eric Sermon and Public Enemy have given rhythm and blues new life by sampling the songs of Marvin Gaye and James Brown. What the black church had a role in creating, hip-hop had a role in bringing to an end. Some in the black church saw soul music as devil music, yet the black church has been the very birthing place for many soul singers. There would be no Ray Charles, Marvin Gaye or Pattie Labelle without the black church. When you look around black culture, you can't help but see the influence of the black church, and when you look around hip-hop culture, which includes the spoken word of rap, you shouldn't be able to deny the fact that there is a God somewhere!

PREACHERS WHO CONNECT—OR DON'T

As a young African American pastor and preacher, I wonder sometimes if the preacher has become disconnected from young people within hip-hop culture. Urban youth have told me on a number of occasions that the preacher speaks to churched adults but not to them or the culture they live in. That seems very different from Paul in the book of Acts, who not only spoke to the various Gentile cultures he encountered but even used their own philosophers to preach truth.

Watching BET, MTV or other channels that appeal to young urban African Americans, I often see hip-hop artists who seem to have these young people in the palm of their hand. As they hold the microphone and blast out passionate words, often raging against the establishment and "how things is," they move and control crowds of mostly black young people, inciting them to dance, cheer, scream and "throw their hands in the air / and wave them like they just don't care."

On the Word Network, a channel that I don't think urban black young people watch, at least not at the time that I'm watching (about 5:30 a.m.), you could view evangelism programs featuring all black preachers just about 24 hours a day, 365 days a year. Basically these shows are black church services on television. These preachers are sweating and screaming, and some are asking for financial support for their sweating and screaming. Some of them are going beyond sweating and screaming to actually proclaim biblical truths that stir me to action. I love this channel because it features some very good expositors who are preaching truth from the Word of God. They are also moving a crowd to "throw their hands in the air," except that those doing the hand waving are also calling out "Amen!" and "Preach!" However, as the camera pans the congregation, often the reaction of the young people is very different. Many times while black adult church folks are very excited and all into the sermon, I see many black youth looking as if they would rather be hearing from a hip-hop artist, someone who speaks more to the issues of their generation than some Reverend Can't-Get-Past-the-Civil-Rights-Movement or Pastor Let's-Get-Rich-Don't-Get-Sick.

There are some great exceptions. Take Pastor Jamal Harrison-Bryant, pastor of the Empowerment Temple in the Baltimore area. He preaches at the intersection of Preacher Avenue and Hip-Hop Street. He knows how to keep an older generation of blacks on board through the use of old-time "whooping" but also to cause young people to jump out of their seats with his use of hip-hop slang. Pastor Harrison-Bryant stands out as one of the few public preachers on the airwaves who seem to understand that the black church is in a battle on the microphone for the ears and hearts of this generation.

Otis Moss III is another who is able to bridge the traditional church crowd and the hip-hop crowd. He is pastor of the historic

Tabernacle Baptist Church in Augusta, Georgia, and serves on the advisory board of the *African American Pulpit.* He is scholarly and very in tune with the black preaching tradition but can pull hip-hop flow into his preaching style with ease.

Now while I'm giving props to preachers who can flow within hip-hop culture, let me diversify the list to include women and non-blacks. There are some preaching sisters out there who are able to hold their own in the pulpit and in hip-hop culture. A few of them are Dr. Rene Rochester of Youth for Christ, Alise Barrymore of North Park University in Chicago, Cecilia Williams of Bethel Seminary in the Twin Cities of Minnesota (I'm biased because she is part of my congregation, but others will tell you, she can preach!) and Justine Connelly of Young Life. Maybe it is because these women spend a lot of time preaching to students that they know how to bridge church and hip-hop.

Bart Campolo is a European American preacher who knows how to preach in the urban setting to the church and to those living in hip-hop. Now it could be because he grew up in Philadelphia and is the son of Tony Campolo (the only white guy I knew growing up who could "bring it" in the black church) that he has developed into another preacher who can bridge the church and hip-hop.

These preachers are bringing the Word of God to the hip-hop generation in a way that moves young people to consider the power and significance of the cross. In hip-hop culture the ability of the emcee to move the crowd is everything. It doesn't matter how good your studio project is; the ability to move the crowd live and on stage is essential. And the stage can be an alleyway, parking lot, basketball court or school bus. What sets the stage is the ability to move a crowd.

The hard question for secular hip-hop culture is, *what* are you attempting to move the crowd to do, if anything? With many of the messages of mainstream hip-hop music still focused on violence as a means to solve conflict, the degrading of women and the glamorization of drug abuse, I'm very concerned about what the crowd does when the show is over. Of course this does not take into account the full depth and diversity of hip-hop culture; here I just want to focus on the negative segment. The powers that be—who in many cases aren't the same skin color as the hip-hop artists themselves—have decided that mainstream hip-hop will actually exploit and degrade the very people of the artists themselves. I wonder why many rappers don't realize this. Maybe the pain of their past, the dreams of fame or in some cases the weed they've been smoking has blinded them to the new plantation and slavery system of the "secular" music industry. It's no longer blacks picking cotton: they themselves and the art form they represent have become the new cotton that is being picked. They are the fabric that is made into clothing that is wrapped around the body of today's youth culture, regardless of race or geography. So could it be that the ones that move the crowd in the mainstream are actually field hands of a corporate slave master who is content with making money and not too concerned about the fact that there are more black men in prison and rehab than in college and on Wall Street?

Now when it comes to moving a crowd to action, what group has a greater heritage than the black preacher? Dr. Martin Luther King Jr. alone serves as the black preacher as the shining example of prophet, motivator, commentator and vocal equipper of a people to rise out of oppression. There is a history of not only crowd-moving but also crowd-changing black preachers in the United States of America. This is not to take anything away from the black intellectuals of our past and present, but many of them would admit that they were in some way inspired by black preaching as well.

Well, what happened then? Why has the most moving and prophetic voice of a people been replaced, at least for young people, by hip-hop culture?

Remember, that culture now includes not only rapping but the resurgence of the "spoken word" (poetry). I think the spoken word takes hip-hop back to its true roots of inspiration from the likes of the Last Poets. Black comedy made a resurgence in the 1990s as well, mostly because of *Def Comedy Jam,* a show that partnered the stage presence of Richard Pryor with the turntables of Grandmaster Flash.

This turns my earlier question around. How in the world can black preachers compete, then, in a handicap match against rappers, poets and comedians for not only the microphone but, more important, the privilege of moving a crowd of black youth to transformation and action? By recognizing that those communication forms not only have something in common with black preaching but to a certain degree are inspired by black preaching. From here, we can move on to examine and observe what it is within the various communication styles—minus the vulgarities—that works. I believe in the end the black preacher can still prove to be the most powerful voice within the community, but we must admit some shortcomings and keep on learning. At its best, black preaching is inspired by God, blending biblical authority with contemporary societal commentary. But there are still some issues that need to be dealt with if preaching is to be more effective in reaching the hip-hop generation.

One, we black preachers have to actually admit that we don't have sole control of the microphone like we once did in the African American community. Back then, because of slavery and Jim Crow, the black preacher was the only free and powerful voice we had to empower our people. Because we couldn't speak as governor or president (it seems we still can't), the black preacher was the closest thing we had to a political voice of power. So how did we lose much of this influence amongst the hip-hop generation? The Reverend Jesse Jackson Sr. has a program on the Word Network, but most of the people joining him in that political awareness and worship experience seem to be people that have been following him since the 1970s. The audience seen on the program doesn't suggest that Reverend Jackson is speaking to the hip-hop generation.

I believe the civil rights movement, especially through Dr. King's voice, was the last time we heard black preaching at its best in its ability to mobilize a generation of young people to move not just from side to side but into action against systems of oppression. Don't get me wrong, today there *are* preachers influencing young lives—but it is not on the national level of King, not only as preacher but as organizer. What happened? Maybe the Last Poets are a good place to start in seeking to understand the battle for the microphone within the black community.

The reason I think the Last Poets are a good place to start is that they represent the roots of hip-hop culture, at least in terms of rap, and also that they came into a place of influence within the black community at a crucial time. I started to think more about the Last Poets when I roomed with Fred Lynch at a youth pastors' conference not long ago. As he played a CD of the Last Poets, I realized the social and political significance of their rap and poetry.

After Martin Luther King Jr. died, the Last Poets took on the challenge of boldly speaking to what was going on among a people enraged over the death of a prophetic and powerful voice. The Last Poets are connected to the black preaching tradition in that their words provided a commentary on what was going on socially at the time. We see the Black CNN once again in their speaking to the ills of inner-city black culture.

I don't intend to give the Last Poets all the credit for the changing of the dominant voice in African American culture. But they represent how the voice changed. Even before Dr. King's assassination, there was a rising movement among emerging African American leaders known as Black Power. This movement included new voices that played a role in the development of the hip-hop voice and were marked, according to Carl F. Ellis Jr. (in his *Free at Last? The Gospel in the African-American Experience*), by secular humanism. These voices included leaders such as Stokely Carmichael and Floyd McKissick.

> The concept of Black Power rests on a fundamental premise: Before a group can enter open society, it must first close ranks. By this time we were also beginning to see some negative effects of our own unrighteousness. If the militant thinkers had a functioning biblical worldview, they could have anticipated this. Thus the closer we came to our goal of overthrowing White oppression, the more our own ungodliness surfaced to oppress us. Negro pimps became Black pimps, Negro dope pushers became Black dope pushers. In the words of the Last Poets, Niggers change into doing Black nigger things.
>
> (ELLIS, *FREE AT LAST?* P. 114)

To me the Last Poets aren't a prophetic voice, they are a voice of commentary, telling things as they see them as they watch the game of black life, oppression, love, pain and death. When you lose the prophetic voice of influence within a generation of young blacks, it can get replaced with a commentary-type voice that attempts to simply give the raw truth of what's going on in the hood. I see "secular" rap artists as commentators and journalists but not prophets. If there are going to be prophet-type rappers, they can come only through the Christian rap community—through Holy Hip-Hop culture.

Holy Hip-Hop emcees provide opportunities to plant a direct

prophetic voice of justice, truth and salvation right in the heart of hip-hop culture. The Ambassador of Cross Movement is one such prophetic hip-hop voice. In the mainstream of hip-hop this prophetic voice is not widely known; hip-hop on a national scale is not aware of a prophetic voice. When there is no prophetic voice that presents the truths of God at a level that young people can understand, often the commentary and journalistic voices get called prophetic voices. An example of how this can play out was the battle for the microphone between preacher and politician Jesse Jackson Sr. and rapper Tupac. Because Reverend Jackson's voice was seen as a prophetic one only among black adults at best, the black youth culture, feeling as if there was no black preacher proclaiming truth at a level they could understand, took a street commentator like Tupac and even in his death deemed him a prophet.

Tupac was not a prophet; he was a commentator, letting us see the raw truth of life in the hood after the black church had ceased to be as proactively involved as it was before and during the civil rights movement. I believe the post-civil rights movement riots marked a time of transition when the prophetic voice of the pulpit lost influence with young blacks and was replaced by street commentator voices of those like the Last Poets, who fueled the rise of hip-hop culture—rappers, poets and comedians who today have greater influence over black youth than preachers do. Let's just be real and admit that black preaching has lost its mass influence among young people and that the microphone has been stolen by rap emcees influencing this youth culture—regardless of race—like never before. This ability for rappers to influence not only black youth, but the youth culture in general is so significant in my theory that this transition of microphone influence is tied into the life and death of Dr. Martin Luther King Jr.

Fred Lynch, pioneer of Holy Hip-Hop, believes that in some ways the roots of hip-hop culture lives out the vision Dr. King laid out in his famous "I Have a Dream" speech. Dr. King spoke of dreaming about a day when young people of all races would join hands and sing of freedom. What movement, outside of hip-hop, is causing youth of all races to join hand in hand today? Hip-hop culture has been able to break down walls that still stand as strongholds within the Christian church.

TAKING THE MICROPHONE BACK!

For the black preacher or any other preacher wanting to reclaim the microphone of influence among this generation of young blacks and others influenced by hip-hop culture, a couple of things must happen. First, the black preacher must develop a theology of God and youth. The Bible is full of stories of God's using young people to do incredible things. From young David to Esther to Timothy, God uses young people to bring about spiritual, political and social change. Even in our contemporary history, we must articulate how much young people have been at the forefront of movements of change.

I believe that, unfortunately, the young people who were active during the civil rights movement have done a poor job of passing on the baton of leadership to the next generation in an integrated society. Hip-hop culture is telling older blacks, "If you are not willing to equip and empower us for leadership, we will take leadership by any means necessary. If the black church won't teach me how to live in this post-civil rights society, and if whites still are not willing to take their hand of oppression off us, then we will—in the words of Shane Price, Minneapolis community activist and head of the African-American's Men's Project—'create a negative cash flow system' to empower ourselves." Both legitimate and illegitimate forms of self-empowerment, whether coming out of high school to play in the NBA, giving up college to pursue a rap career (legitimate) or selling drugs (illegitimate), are corporate rages against a machine of oppression and against the black church's catering to old folks rather than reaching and raising up a generation of urban black youth.

So preachers and other Christian speakers must make proactive efforts to connect biblical stories with the issues, barriers and challenges of urban youth. The book of Esther, for example, must be preached in view of the urban girl who is not being raised by her biological mother or father, who is not of the dominant race, who is judged only by her physical features, yet God raises her up to bring about spiritual and political change. We must dare every Sunday to preach to the youth within hip-hop culture.

Earlier I mentioned Holy Hip-Hop artist Fred Lynch and his creation of *The Epic,* a hip-hop translation of the Gospel of John that communicates biblical truth using the language of hip-hop. Fred uses hip-hop language but takes care not to water down the gospel truth. In the book's introduction he explains why he created *The Epic:*

> From my early teenage years of rappin the gospel out on the streets some 20 years ago to the present I have seen enthusiasm and excitement about the message when God's Word is magnified through rhythm and rhyme. God has literally taken what I was doing on the forgotten street corners of the inner city and birthed a vision to spread His word to a searching generation. . . . *The Epic* portrays the gospel from the Book of John in a contemporary format. Language is where it starts, and Rap-Rhythm and Poetry is the language of the street, where Jesus lived and taught.

The Epic is an essential resource in the library of any preacher with a passion to bring the gospel message to those living in hip-hop culture.

While staying committed to its ghetto roots, hip-hop has had a broader impact within an integrated society. Hip-hop culture has kept a strong black base within the youth culture, but by "keeping it real" it has reached out to and influenced a multiethnic mass of young people. The reason rap is the number-one music genre right now is that not only are blacks into it but whites just can't stop buying either. Remember too the roots of hip-hop as a multiethnic movement of young people in places like the Bronx, New York.

The black church must take on the challenge of proclaiming a word from God that not only unashamedly speaks to this generation of young blacks but also influences the youth culture in general. The black preacher on the microphone should be a prophetic voice that not only speaks to and moves the crowd of his own youth but speaks to the youth culture at large. Now, to a certain extent this can be done simply by speaking to the issues facing young black males. I believe that black boys are the most influential tribe within the youth culture. Black boys are rapping, starring in movies, leaving high school to play in the NBA, signing multi-million-dollar shoe contracts, and selling everything from Sprite to Nike to McDonald's. If black preachers would develop a theology of God and youth, interweave it into their preaching and follow up with proactive ministry models, they could dominate the microphone of this generation of urban youth and most likely the youth culture at large.

The next way the black preacher could dominate the microphone among this generation of young people is by dealing head on with sexism. Hip-hop still is diseased by its degrading and exploitation of women. And to be honest, some of the history of the urban church in this area is not much better. If the black preacher would develop a theology of the empowerment of women through a broader reading of Scripture that lifts up girls and women as prophets, deacons, preachers and prayer warriors, it would send a powerful message to this generation of young girls who are searching for love, identity, meaning and real relationships. Hip-hop from an emcee standpoint is still dominated by men, and with the exception of Queen Latifah and Missy Elliott, female emcees have to present themselves in a very sexual way to be accepted in the mainstream, as Lil' Kim and Foxy Brown have done. The black preacher must speak to the woman as leader, and the male black preacher must be about the further empowerment of the female preacher on the microphone.

The black preacher must also embrace the Christian hip-hop community, which if coupled with their preaching could be a powerful force of evangelism and discipleship among this generation of young people. It's a shame that were it not for white evangelical venues, most Christian rap groups would have no place to minister. The black church must fully embrace Christian rap now as a vehicle of ministry to young people. I love having a Christian emcee as part of our worship experience on Sunday morning. I believe it sends a message to those living in hip-hop culture that there is a place for them in the kingdom. A strictly traditional worship experience can isolate and ignore the very people you may be trying to reach on Sunday morning. The future of the black church depends on this, in my opinion.

Finally, we must remember the source of our preaching as the true prophetic voice of empowerment within the African American community. Whenever this voice is not relevant to the youth among us, the prophetic voice coming from the church will be replaced by the street voice of commentary within secular hip-hop culture. There is no need for the preacher to allow the mainstream hip-hop emcee to be the dominant voice for young people in hip-hop culture. A prophetic voice can make a major difference in the lives of youth.

I've been blessed of God to have opportunities on a regular basis to speak to the hip-hop generation and find favor with them.

There are a number of reasons for this favor. One, preaching is indeed my calling, and calling does matter. Two, there must be a dependence on God and a belief that indeed God desires to speak to those in hip-hop culture. Two, there must be a willingness to study the major issues of hip-hop culture as well as build authentic relationships with those living in it. Finally, one must understand that this approach to preaching is not new to those connected to the black preaching tradition. The black preaching tradition has always connected the Word of God with contemporary culture and the issues, barriers and challenges our people face within it. Our task as prophetic preachers of today is to grab the microphone, step into hip-hop culture and continue the tradition.

8

THE Deejay AND THE WORSHIP LEADER

As I was growing up, I was significantly influenced by the hip-hop element of the deejay. My earliest experience of being affected and infected by the deejay came from my uncle Xavier. Xavier is my mom's only and younger brother. Growing up with five sisters, three older and two younger, had to be a challenge. By the time I came on the scene, Uncle Xavier was living in the basement of my grandmother's house, and I didn't realize it then but he was very immersed in hip-hop. He was a deejay of sorts and frequently would blast music from his turntables and what seemed to me at the time an incredible sound system. He was really into music and took seriously his sound system, from which he filled the whole house with the soulful sounds of Stevie Wonder and the funk sounds of Earth, Wind and Fire as well as George Clinton, Rick James and Prince. My uncle, D.J. X, as I will call him in this chapter, didn't use all the more esoteric skills of the deejay such as scratching and cutting, but he was solid with blending and basic mixing. He had a good feel for what song should come next, when to slow it down and when to change the mood from strictly "let's party" to "let's think."

When D.J. X was in the basement filling the house with sound, I couldn't help but be drawn in. When I heard the music,

I would either go down to where he was or just sit on the stairs and listen. I was enraptured by the soulful and funky sounds. Pictures, stories and daydreams filled my head as I listened. Stevie Wonder's sounds are what I remember most; even though the sounds of James Brown have a heavy influence on hip-hop, I believe the lyrics of Stevie Wonder should get more credit than they usually do. His lyrics had such a great range, from "I Wish," taking up everyday issues of the urban African American family, to "Higher Ground," giving both social and spiritual commentary. A similar range of complex issues, barriers and challenges is reflected today in the diverse and complex styles of rap. My uncle had the ability to blend and mix music that made me want to dance, want to think, want to dream and even made me want to worship.

I have no idea if my uncle was operating according to well-thought-out concepts or just by natural instinct. At large family gatherings, whether it be a family reunion or wedding reception, D.J. X could be seen on the turntables. He deejayed house parties as well as other functions. As he grew older, graduated from college and went into corporate America, he left the life of the deejay. I wonder whether in his house in suburban Woodbury, Minnesota, he ever still gets the itch to get on the turntables and fill the house with sound.

I was blessed to grow up with music. Thinking about the influence my uncle had on me through his deejaying leads me to reflect on other members of my family who were deejays of sorts themselves. On Saturdays when I was a kid, my father would turn on the stereo and stack up 45s. As they dropped, he sat at the dining-room table snapping his fingers, putting on a small house party just for our family. My dad, Forice Smith, though not a singer or musician as such, was a resident deejay who introduced me to the blues, soul and funk. I learned of B. B. King, the Ohio Players,

Bobby Womack, James Brown and many others through my day, my personal Saturday afternoon deejay.

My older brother Fontez is the one I truly give credit to for my introduction to rap music and hip-hop culture. When I was in middle school, he would have me mix tapes featuring various hip-hop groups. Fontez was my hip-hop supplier; on a monthly basis he gave me all I needed to become a hip-hop head, by moving from the songs on the mix tapes to explore other elements of hip-hop.

Other family members too were very musical, whether playing the role of deejay at barbecues, family house parties and family reunions, or providing mix tapes to further immerse me in hip-hop culture.

I also grew up with a mother and grandmothers on both sides who were gospel singers in the church and had the ability to lead people into praise and worship on any given Sunday. This influenced my involvement in various choirs, praise teams and gospel groups. My mother. Sandra Smith, as well as my grandmothers, Mary Smith and Alice Jean Knight, could walk into a church, step up into a choir loft and lead people into the presence of God in a powerful way.

HOW THE DEEJAY WORKS

Having grown up in both hip-hop and the church, I see connections between the hip-hop deejay and the worship leader. Let's begin exploring these connections by looking closely at the functions of the deejay. Many hip-hop heads believe the deejay to be the mother element of hip-hop that gave birth to the other elements.

Hip-hop can trace its history back to the 1970s, the age of disco and the beginning of what hip-hop writer Nelson George calls the emergence of "postsoul." To a certain degree, talking about a postsoul, post-civil rights age puts the subject of postmodernism into an African American, urban and multiethnic context. The reason it is important to recognize the roots of hip-hop in the age of disco is that disco became popular through its tie-in with the dance club, and the main attraction and leader at the dance club is the deejay. The deejay has the job of leading people into dance, of getting people excited and ready to party. Having a good time at a party or a dance club has a lot to do with who the deejay is and what skills he or she brings to the table. African American, Latino and Island youth culture took the role of the deejay to a whole new level in the 1970s and set the stage for a new movement known as hip-hop.

Deejays such as Kool Herc, Grandmaster Flash and Afrika Bambaataa are the pioneers of hip-hop. Hip-hop begins with the deejay, and thus the deejay is hip-hop's foundational element. The deejay brings the music and the spirit of hip-hop to the crowd.

I grew up around the deejay. At school parties, the deejay was there. At the roller-skating rink, the deejay was there. At my grandmother's house, there was my uncle the deejay. At the high school basketball game, there was the deejay for the halftime show. During those years the deejay was everywhere except the church. The deejay caused me to want to party. The deejay assisted me in connecting to that special girl. The deejay helped me learn the words to many songs. It is the deejay's job to create an atmosphere that influences the crowd in a significant way.

In the church's gospel music as well as praise and worship music, there are leaders as well. Their job is to lead the congregation into the worship of God. In the African American urban church especially, this is a major role. The choir director traditionally has been very influential in the African American church. The soloist in the choir is very influential as well. In the contemporary African American urban church, this role is taken up by the worship leader. The worship leader and the preacher are key components of the African American urban church, just as the deejay and the emcee are key components of hip-hop culture. Let's see how this works in some models of hip-hop worship within the emerging African American urban church.

INCORPORATING THE DEEJAY INTO WORSHIP

One model to be considered is the deejay as an emerging worship leader within a hip-hop church. I first saw this model at the Urban Youth Workers Institute, which is put on every year in California. The founder and leader of this conference is Dr. Larry Acosta. He uses the deejay in a unique way in the conference. Outside on the mall, as people are moving to various workshops and seminars, a deejay is set up with speakers blasting Holy Hip-Hop. The music sets the mood for the conference. It causes people to move their head from side to side as they walk. You can have a mobile urban hip-hop praise and worship experience as you go into a seminar to learn principles of urban youth ministry. In the general sessions of the conference, the deejay sets the mood as people are gathering and supports the praise and worship band. Recently at this conference, an alternative praise and worship band included a deejay in its worship set.

The hip-hop element of the deejay can be used to lead praise and worship. Maybe your church doesn't have the resources to have a hip-hop praise and worship band, but you have someone with the skills to deejay. A deejay, playing instrumental tracks, could arrange hip-hop praise and worship lyrics for the congregation to sing during youth service or a Sunday morning hip-hop service.

Another model involves using the deejay not as the worship leader but as a part of the worship band. Worship and youth ministry leaders Stacey and Trynese Jones, along with deejay Charles Albritton, use this model in youth services they have developed for Citadel Church of God in Christ in Brooklyn Park, Minnesota. The deejay plays the instrumental version of a known song in hip-hop, or because of the access deejays have to music, underground instrumental tracks could be used. Trynese Jones is an exceptional writer, singer and arranger who works with the deejay to take traditional hymns and turn them into hip-hop worship songs; she also writes original hip-hop praise songs. I preached at a youth service where the deejay was used in this way in the praise and worship at Citadel. As Deejay Charles mixed an instrumental hip-hop track by Lucy Pearl, Trynese, Stacey and other vocalists sang a very catchy tune, "We Come to Worship." The rest of the praise and worship band included two organists and a drummer.

I've seen another version of this model at the youth workers convention put on by Youth Specialties in Tampa in 2002. At this conference Pastor Tommy Kyllonen of Crossover Community Church led a hip-hop worship experience that included a deejay, break dancers and emcees. This was the first time I had seen a hip-hop church up close. It was truly an incredible experience and so exciting to see hip-hop artists using the talents for the kingdom of God. Not only was Crossover Community Church the first hip-hop church in the country, but it also is very committed to equipping other churches to engage hip-hop culture. It has a couple of websites that are very helpful in equipping the church to develop hip-hop praise and worship within the Sunday morning service or a youth service.

The final model that I will share in this chapter doesn't include the deejay at all but what I will call the emerging hip-hop urban worship leader. This model is best seen in the hip-hop praise and worship ministry of Urban Street Level, led by Elwood and Betty Jones. The band led by Elwood Jones, who is a bass player, primarily mixes the sounds of the Ohio Players, Kool and the Gang, and Chuck Brown with the hip-hop sounds of the Roots, Dr. Dre and Sean "P. Diddy" Combs. To truly understand what I'm talking about, you have to purchase the CDs *Urban Street Level Live* and *Urban Street Level Live 2*. These two are the funkiest praise and worship projects I've ever heard, and they point to what I believe praise and worship should be like in the emerging African American urban church. Urban Street Level takes contemporary praise and worship songs such as "Breathe," "Open the Eyes of My Heart" and "Let the Walls Fall Down" and puts them to hip-hop and neo-soul beats in a live band. Betty Jones, a veteran praise and worship leader in the local church, pulls in traditional church people, but she shows that she has a great heart for the hip-hop generation through her hip-hop slang, dress and energy. Urban Street Level's use of hip-hop and other urban contemporary sounds doesn't water down the gospel, as some fear could be the case. Instead they bring a very creative praise and worship style that reaches people already in the church, connects with unchurched people living in hip-hop culture and puts on a hip-hop praise party all at the same time.

In the mid 1990s Urban Street Level added Sherrie Jones, a vocalist who is a worship leader in her own right. In fall 2003 Sherrie became the worship leader at my church. In many ways she models what a worship leader in the emerging hip-hop urban church should be about. She loves the Lord and desires to use a relevant sound to lead people into an atmosphere of worship. Our praise and worship style at the Sanctuary Covenant Church, like that of Urban Street Level, involves using hip-hop, soul and alternative sounds and putting this sound to hymns such as "How Great Thou Art" and "Sweet, Sweet Presence of Jesus," as well as contemporary praise and worship standards. We desire to have a praise and worship party that connects to those who are already Christian in our congregation but also hooks those who are coming back to or connecting to the church for the first time and living in hip-hop urban culture. We also desire to hook youth in our Sunday morning worship experience. Our band leader, Troy Williams, plays keyboards and saxophone, and in the spirit of 1970s and 1980s soul, which influences hip-hop to a certain extent, he puts together a band on a weekly basis that includes guitar, bass, drums, keyboards and sometimes a horn section. Sherrie Jones, as the worship experience leader, leads praise and worship on most Sundays along with about six other vocalists. From time to time she incorporates an emcee or rapper into the mix.

The purpose is to provide a weekly worship experience that is relevant in reaching unchurched people in the inner-city community of North Minneapolis and beyond. This is a multiethnic hip-hop community. We have found that our style of worship has also been effective in reaching people of various ethnicities who already consider themselves Christian and come out of a more traditional church experience. Our congregation is at least 50 percent European American, yet our style of praise and worship has not been a turnoff to them. Now, I'm not going to say that everyone who attends our church just loves our worship style, but it seems that they are sold on our mission and understand why we worship the way we do.

The key is the worship leader. Sherrie has a very inviting personality. Her joy and excitement are contagious, and she lovingly draws people into our style of worship. She has a way of making sure that people know that what we do is beyond performance and is truly a new and creative way of expressing our love for God and connecting to God's overwhelming love for us.

Of course it takes resources to put on this kind of praise and worship experience, but in the context of our mission it is well worth it. Deciding on this or any other model of hip-hop praise and worship has to begin with a sense of mission and purpose. Our purpose statement at the Sanctuary Covenant Church is "to reconcile the people of the city to God and one another." One of our core values for accomplishing our purpose is a "worship experience which is multi-ethnic, multi-sensory, and relevant using hip-hop, soul, and alternative elements."

If it's going to engage hip-hop culture, the church can't be afraid to see the praise and worship experience as a "Holy Ghost party." The worship leader is in charge of getting the spiritual party started and must be willing to use elements of hip-hop culture to pull churched people into the mission of engaging culture without feeling that this compromises their ability to enter into worship for themselves and at the same time to hook unchurched people. For our church, praise and worship is for anybody and everybody, not just church folks. Everyone is invited to enter in to the praise party.

In my years of going to hip-hop parties of all kinds, the deejay always desired that everyone had a good time. The worst feeling for a deejay is the one that comes from playing music while people stand against the wall, not dancing, not getting into it. That is an unsuccessful party. A successful party is when everyone is on the dance floor. A successful praise and worship experience involves connecting as many people as you can, regardless of their background, to a community of worship at a level they can understand. The worship leader, like the deejay, ought to desire that everyone join in the party. The difference in the Holy Ghost party is that the worship leader, in a loving and inviting manner, seeks to introduce everyone at the party to the guest of honor, Jesus Christ.

BRINGING Hip-Hop
INTO YOUR WORSHIP SERVICE

There is influence and power in hip-hop culture and music. There is also influence and power in prayer, praise and worship.

Many find it easy to paint a picture of how these two forms are in direct opposition to each other. A committed Christian may see hip-hop culture and its music as betraying the influence of the devil, while prayer, praise and worship are strictly the vehicles God calls us to use to give him praise. Some are confident that they can easily tell the difference between what music is of the devil and what is of God; they tend to come to the conclusion that there is no way that hip-hop music can be of God, especially if the lyrics are violent, degrading to women and include a lot of vulgar language. The case could also be made that hip-hop culture and music are of the devil because the beats are more reminiscent of the nightclub and the urban street house party than of the church choir or revival. In contrast, praise and worship seem to be clearly of God. These folks have made up in their mind about what the elements of true praise and worship are—things like hymns, the organ, spirituals, an acoustic guitar or a choir. And they must occur within the broader spectrum of a worship service, all followed up by preaching.

But seeing through this limited lens to conclude that hip-hop culture and music are of the devil and praise and worship are of God puts the two in a position of opposition, and we are left with no opportunity to think through the history they share or the potential there might be to blend elements from both to reach out to those within hip-hop culture for purposes of further building God's kingdom.

This view must be challenged biblically and theologically before we bring hip-hop elements into the church worship experience. So before we look at how to bring hip-hop into the worship experience of the church, let's look more closely at why the church might be totally against this notion.

CHURCH OPPOSITION TO HIP-HOP

The "hip-hop as evil versus traditional praise worship as holy" approach to music and culture is held by many church people I've talked to over the years. They see hip-hop music as worldly. They can even quote Scripture to defend their judgment—for example, the following text: "But avoid worldly and empty chatter, for it will lead to further ungodliness, and their talk will spread like gangrene" (2 Timothy 2:16-17). Those who have heard only hip-hop lyrics that celebrate violence, degrade women or use vulgar language may see hip-hop music as "worldly chatter." The only influence and power that would be seen in it is the power to lead listeners into a life of "further ungodliness." Rap is seen from this standpoint as the talk that spreads its negativity like gangrene. Some make direct ties between hip-hop music and youth crime, sexually transmitted diseases, out-of-wedlock pregnancies and what is deemed inappropriate fashion. Hip-hop music, like earlier music forms such as rock and roll and metal, get blamed by certain people as responsible for at-risk behavior.

Though this kind of influence is blown out of proportion at times, I do recognize the power and influence of the arts, including music. I believe that music can influence behavior, both negatively and positively. Here, though, my point is that someone who sees hip-hop music as "worldly chatter" considers its power and influence to be only ungodly and would not find any value in using it within the worship experience of the church.

Others who don't have "hip-hop ears" could see rap as "empty chatter" for another reason. If you didn't grow up in hip-hop, it can be hard to understand the lyrics, so it sounds like meaningless noise. My parents didn't grow up in hip-hop, so it's hard for them to get much meaning and sense out of hip-hop music. I, on the other hand, grew up with the beginnings of hip-hop, so I totally understood what was being said by the early pioneers of rap. Later on, though, new styles of hip-hop music came on the scene and the culture expanded. By the time the Dirty South style came on the scene, for example, with artist such as David Banner, Bone Crusher, Nelly and Lil' Flip, I was already an adult. I didn't grow up in this style of hip-hop, so it's hard for me to understand. To me it sounds like empty chatter, but young people today who grew up in that understand it clearly. It's easy to understand, then, why older church folks would see hip-hop music in general as not really saying anything.

Some older adults I know who aren't in the church don't believe that hip-hop music is saying anything in comparison to the music of artists and groups they grew up with, like Marvin Gaye, Aretha Franklin, the Doobie Brothers, Earth, Wind and Fire, and the Isley Brothers. If anything, they might connect hip-hop music to artists of the 1970s like George Clinton and Parliament/Funkadelic—fans back in the day say you had to be high on drugs to really get into what they were talking about.

If we believe that rap is empty chatter and really isn't saying anything worthwhile, we will naturally conclude that any actual hip-hop influence would be either minimal or worthless.

Putting all this together, you can see the great challenge I face in developing a theology of hip-hop culture that can help motivate the church to bring hip-hop into the worship experience. When we see hip-hop music and culture totally in a negative light, we assume that hip-hop is worldly and that its influence is ungodly. This could lead to seeing hip-hop as idolatrous, as the enemy, as being used solely to advance the agenda of the devil.

This perspective reminds me of the 1 Kings 18 account of a confrontation between the prophet of God, Elijah, and the prophets of Baal on Mount Carmel: "Elijah came near to all the people and said, 'How long will you hesitate between two opinions? If the LORD is God, follow Him; but if Baal, follow him.' But the people did not answer him a word" (1 Kings 18:21). Seeing hip-hop music as negative and worldly sets it up against the church worship experience—the choir, the praise and worship team, the preaching. It becomes the music of Baal verses the music and preaching of God: two "opinions" between which we must choose.

Elijah gets into a confrontation with the prophets of Baal to see who really is following the one powerful and true God. "Then Elijah said to the people, 'I alone am left a prophet of the LORD, but Baal's prophets are 450 men'" (1 Kings 18:22). As the hip-hop community boasts a strong influence and a global movement, those in the church could see themselves as standing alone in bringing truth to young people today, see themselves as Elijah and the philosophers of hip-hop as the prophets of Baal.

In that case we have a confrontation between good and evil, God and hip-hop, just as Elijah challenges the prophets of Baal to a contest of sorts to prove the power of their gods: "'Then you call on the name of your god, and I will call on the name of the LORD, and the God who answers by fire, He is God.' And all the people said, 'That is a good idea'" (1 Kings 18:24).

When we make these sorts of parallels, you can see how many

churches might have a theology and mindset in place that would make it difficult to embrace hip-hop as a ministry method, especially on Sunday morning. Still, I want to dig deeper and show why it is important for the church to use elements of the culture that surrounds it within the worship service, even if this culture is seen as "pagan."

RESPONDING TO "PAGAN" CULTURE

If we were to accept hip-hop culture as a pagan culture, we would still have to consider how the early church presented the gospel in pagan culture. We have a history to look to in which the church takes what is pagan and uses it to point to Christ. Take the celebration of Easter, for example. A quick search on the Internet led me to "The Easter Page: Traditions, History and Dates of Easter." It states the following:

> Easter was originally a pagan festival. The ancient Saxons celebrated the return of spring with an uproarious festival commemorating their goddess of offspring and of springtime, Eastre. When the second-century Christian missionaries encountered the tribes of the north with their pagan celebrations, they attempted to convert them to Christianity. They did so, however, in a clandestine manner. It would have been suicide for the very early Christian converts to celebrate their holy days with observances that did not coincide with celebrations that already existed. To save lives, the missionaries cleverly decided to spread their religious message slowly throughout the populations by allowing them to continue to celebrate pagan feasts, but to do so in a Christian manner.

So Easter, the holiest of holidays in the American church, actually began as a pagan celebration in European culture. This pagan celebration was altered by missionaries in order to be used to advance God's kingdom within the culture. Why shouldn't we treat hip-hop culture in some similar fashion, using elements and founding principles of hip-hop to proclaim Jesus Christ as Lord and Savior? When we treat hip-hop as only demonic or pagan, we lose this opportunity of evangelism and outreach.

Now don't get me wrong: I believe that there is a side to hip-hop that cannot be defended by the church as godly. But that is not all of what hip-hop is. There are some hip-hop songs that do *not* degrade women and that question violence as a primary means to solve conflict. The artists who created them may or may not be Christians.

Unfortunately, there are some "fence-sitting" hip-hop artists, though, who on the same CD rap about Jesus and then turn around and glorify illegal drug use. To me they resemble those people in the 1 Kings 18 account who are hesitating between two opinions. Still, at the same time there are Christian hip-hop artists totally committed to Christ. How do we explain that if we take the position that hip-hop is completely worldly? And what about social consciousness hip-hop that deals with issues of injustice?

STEPS TOWARD CONNECTING HIP-HOP AND WORSHIP

My hope is that we can get beyond seeing hip-hop culture as the enemy in order that hip-hop music might be used as a vehicle of power and influence to advance God's kingdom. Urban minister Bob Hepburn wisely says:

> I'm not saying that in order to minister to the rap/street culture one needs to like rap music, nor am I saying that one needs to agree with everything that's said by the various artists. Nor does one need to condone the things that are wrong with their lifestyles. . . . Yet one can find threads of Biblical truth woven into its fabric, if we look for them (Prov.

25:2). . . . While some believers may question using so secular a phenomenon to discover cultural truths for spiritual ends, the apostle Paul quoted several of the secular poets of his day to reach unbelievers (Epimenides and Aratus are both quoted in Acts 17:28), and believers alike (Menander is quoted in 1 Cor. 15:33 and Epimenides again in Titus 1:12). From a missions perspective, what better way is there to understand the mindset of a people than to study its artists—especially when they are striving to retain the people group's unique cultural identity in art form?

("RAP MUSIC: GIVE ME MY RESPECT, MAN," *URBAN MISSION,* SEPTEMBER 1992, P. 16)

The only place where I might disagree with Hepburn is in his use of the word *secular.* I'm still trying to understand the use of this word among churched people (you may have noticed that throughout this book it appears between quotation marks). The word is used to distinguish godly from ungodly music. But what really makes a song godly or ungodly? Is a song godly just because the lyrics say a lot about Jesus? This issue came to the fore in regard to the Kanye West song "Jesus Walks." Because the song's lyrics speak so much about Jesus, a Christian awards organization wanted to nominate the single for an award. But when the organization folks found out that the song was on a project that was deemed "secular," they withdrew the nomination.

Another thing: I haven't been able to find the word *secular* in the Bible. Does the Bible make the same statements about music that we Christians make when using the term *secular?*

I tend to believe that music is like culture; it is not in itself secular or sacred. I would suppose that at times a certain piece can become secular or sacred based on the heart and motives of the artist as expressed in the lyrical content. But some Christians believe that even instrumental beats can be sacred or secular, and that is hard for me to buy. Then again, if certain video images or lyrics are put to an instrumental beat, the piece as a whole can become positive or negative.

The point is that painting all of hip-hop culture as secular may hinder the church in engaging it for kingdom purposes. Even if some believers consider hip-hop culture to be secular, this should not lead them to see it as created by Satan. Ultimately, I know only one Creator, and that is God and his Son Jesus and the Holy Spirit, who are one within the creation process. Satan may use music, but I don't give him credit as a creator of music or any other art form. For instance, I don't give Satan credit as a creator of movies, but he can use movies as a platform to advocate pornography or violence as a primary means to solve conflict. I don't give Satan credit for hip-hop, but I notice daily how Satan uses hip-hop. My job is to counter this by using hip-hop for kingdom purposes.

The church ought to see itself in a battle with Satan for those within hip-hop culture, not see itself in battle against hip-hop itself. When we use hip-hop for praise and worship in the church service and combine it with other art forms including preaching, members of the hip-hop community can experience the good news at a level they truly can understand. Is this not what missions is all about, bringing Jesus into the culture of a people group? How can we bring Jesus into a culture if we see that culture as only the creation of Satan?

THE POWER OF PRAISE

In scriptural accounts sometimes music is used as a weapon of warfare. In the book of Joshua, we read about the Israelites, after decades out of slavery, finally on the verge of crossing into the Promised Land by way of Jericho. God instructs them through Joshua on how they are to take the land that has been promised to them. Joshua represents a younger generation, with Moses, the old leader, having died. (Reminds me of how hip-hop was formed by a younger generation as the Motown sound was dying out in the mid-1970s.) God's plan for the Israelites' going into the Promised Land includes blowing trumpets, marching and shouting.

The LORD said to Joshua, "See, I have given Jericho into your hand, with its king and the valiant warriors. You shall march around the city, all the men of war circling the city once. You shall do so for six days. Also seven priests shall carry trumpets of rams' horns before the ark; then on the seventh day you shall march around the city seven times, and the priests shall blow the trumpets. It shall be that when they make a long blast with the ram's horn, and when you hear the sound of the trumpet, all the people shall shout with a great shout; and the wall of the city will fall down flat, and the people will go up every man straight ahead."

(JOSHUA 6:2-5)

I get images of marching bands on historic African American college campuses. The unique Afrocentric marching-band style was brought to the big screen through the hip-hop movie *Drum Line,* which shows us how African American marching bands have evolved now that a hip-hop generation is making up the student body on these campuses.

Now let's go back to the book of Joshua. The Israelites are commanded by God to go into the Promised Land with loud praising, shouting, marching and blowing of trumpets, and the result is the walls of the city tumbling down. With this picture in mind, we must ask ourselves, is music influential and powerful because of the influencer Satan or because of the Creator God? I believe because of the Creator God. Even in Exodus the deliverance from slavery is followed up by a worship song. There is a connection between song and deliverance.

Mary, the mother of Jesus, after finding out that she is pregnant with the ultimate Deliverer, begins to worship in song. During slavery, the spirituals were not just music but also code music for freedom from slavery itself. Harriet Tubman, a great woman who led the Underground Railroad, was called Black Moses, as she used spirituals as freedom tools.

There is power in praise and worship. Music's power doesn't begin with the influence of Satan but begins with the Creator God. Why would the church not use a contemporary art form as a tools of power and influence to build God's kingdom—an art form that has become a cultural movement itself?

In the book of Acts, Paul and Silas are put in prison, and while there they begin to sing hymns and pray. Not only are the locks on the jail doors broken open, but others around them give their lives to God!

When they had struck them with many blows, they threw them into prison, commanding the jailer to guard them securely; and he, having received such a command, threw them into the inner prison and fastened their feet in the stocks. But about midnight Paul and Silas were praying and singing hymns of praise to God, and the prisoners were listening to them; and suddenly there came a great earthquake, so that the foundations of the prison house were shaken; and immediately all the doors were opened, and everyone's chains were unfastened.

(ACTS 16:23-26)

There is power in music; there is influence and power in praise and worship. The church must consider the potential of hip-hop praise and worship and the influence it can have among those living in hip-hop culture.

A complete transformation of praise and worship might be too much for some churches, but it should not be too much to at least consider using elements of hip-hop culture within the church. If you have a praise dance team in your church, you are already using an element of hip-hop culture. Now you may argue, "That's not using an element of hip-hop; we have a praise dance team because praise dancing is in the Bible." My response would be "Exactly!" The whole point here is that some elements of hip-hop culture really are rooted in the Bible, because the God whom the Bible deals with is ultimately the Creator of these elements. Given this, how can we not see that the church, especially the African American urban church, is in a prime position to minister to those in hip-hop culture?

At the Sanctuary Covenant Church we use elements of hip-hop within our praise and worship. I wouldn't call my church a hip-hop church, but by engaging the arts and using dance, multimedia, rap and theater in our worship, we are able to provide an environment conducive for reaching an unchurched urban community. The urban church of the future ought to be open to casual urban dress, and to a deejay, rap and spoken word used as vehicles to present the gospel of Jesus Christ to the unchurched hip-hop community. Later I will say more about our approach to the worship experience, but I want to revisit Crossover Community Church because it is a full-fledged hip hop church.

DESIGNING WORSHIP IN A HIP-HOP CONTEXT
Pastor Tommy Kyllonen of Crossover Community Church in Tampa Bay, Florida, is mindful of youth and hip-hop culture when planning his church's weekly worship experience. He explains this in an article in his *Fla. Fest* magazine:

In the past few years, we have begun to do things differently at Crossover. And in 2004, we implemented plans to raise our [preaching] series to the next level. In the process, we continue to discover what works. At the beginning of the year, we set in motion a weekly creative planning meeting that included some of our key staff and leaders. . . . Our team also looked at some of the circumstances that people were talking about in our current culture. We looked at how we could tie that in with a series to get people's attention, while demonstrating the timeless power of God's word. . . . The gospel isn't boring, but many times the way we present it can be! The church as a whole still doesn't understand that people now learn differently; they have shorter attention spans, and they learn more visually today!

(RELEVANT MESSAGE SERIES, NOVEMBER 2004)

Pastor Tommy looks at how the urban church can use hip-hop within the worship experience. His church's design-team approach to Sunday morning worship includes researching issues of current culture. At the Sanctuary Covenant Church we use this model as well. The design-team approach, also referred to as creative design, has been put on the national scene through churches such as Willow Creek Community Church outside Chicago and Ginghamsburg United Methodist Church in the Dayton, Ohio, area. What the hip-hop church does is contextualize this approach to worship to reach a hip-hop urban audience. For this contextualization to take place, the pastor and team must be willing to study hip-hop culture.

As a pastor, I not only pay attention to current issues in hip-hop culture but also study those who are communicating to hip-hop culture and seem to be having an impact. I pay attention to rappers, comedians and spoken-word artists, especially those who seem to be speaking to a multicultural and intergenerational crowd. What I learn affects the way that I preach and the way we design other elements of our worship experience. This research isn't my primary tool for sermon preparation, for that is prayer and Bible study, but it is a significant tool that I use to improve my ability to communicate to those who are unchurched and live in hip-hop culture. One of the goals for the worship experience at my church is that our services be Christ centered yet relevant to an urban, multiethnic hip-hop community. In order to do this we bring elements of hip-hop culture into our worship experience.

Our worship design team meets every Wednesday morning. The team is made up of our worship leader, another staff person who is responsible for communications and media, and me, along with some lay members who are involved in the arts full time. We open up with prayer and share our thoughts about the previous Sunday's service. After that I share with the team what God has put on my heart to preach the next Sunday. This moves us into further prayer, after which we begin to design the service for the coming Sunday. Not only do we want to come up with creative ideas that tie in to the theme of the sermon, but we also want to do it in a way that reaches a hip-hop, multiethnic urban community. We realize that using elements of hip-hop is a crucial ministry method to make this happen, so hip-hop in some form makes it into our worship experience on a regular basis. This doesn't mean there is rap every week. Hip-hop can be present in our worship experience in any of a number of ways. We may have the band play the instrumental track to a hip-hop song while we sing praise and worship lyrics over it. We may have dancers doing hip-hop dance during praise and worship. We may include a spoken-word piece right before the sermon. These are all creative ways to use hip-hop elements that we pray through on any given Wednesday morning in the design team meeting.

We are committed to doing a full-fledged hip-hop service on a Sunday morning once every other month. In this service we pull together the elements that we may have used by themselves in other services. Whether by themselves or all together again, our goal is to reach those living in hip-hop culture who are not yet Christians. For this to work, it is important to use people who are gifted in hip-hop. Those ministering must bring a spirit of excellence and a respect for the art form. People don't rap at our church just because they approach us and say they can. People must audition to become part of the worship team at our church, because we truly want this to be about calling and giftedness.

We have a basic order of worship that begins with praise and worship, a greeting and meeting time, announcements, offering with special music or maybe a dance or theater piece, and then the sermon. We look for ways to bring elements of hip-hop into this structure. In our desire to be creative, from time to time we have deviated from this flow of service. We desire to present the gospel each week in a way that is relevant in the context of our inner-city community.

Now you may be in the right community and have the people in your congregation right now to bring hip-hop into your worship experience. If this is the case, I encourage you to go for it! For some churches, though, it may be most appropriate not in the general worship service but in a youth service. Where this is the case, a hip-hop worship experience can be a model of being a church within a church.

Still other churches, though, may come to the conclusion that now is just not the right time to bring hip-hop into worship services. I encourage you not to bring unneeded division into your church. At this time maybe you should start with prayer, seeking God for what it will take for your church to reach out to unchurched youth and young adults living in hip-hop culture. Believe that God can provide a unique model for what your church can do. Again, there are ways to introduce hip-hop in the church one element at a time. Maybe on a youth Sunday a young person could recite original poetry. Maybe you could start a hip-hop praise team that could dance on a Sunday morning. One way to accustom your church to a hip-hop service is not to call it a hip-hop service. Let it come across as simply the youth ministering to the adults of the church. Many adults in the church, even if they don't especially like the artistic expressions of young people, love to see young people using their gifts to glorify God. Allowing youth to lead within the worship experience could be a great avenue for bringing hip-hop into the life of the church.

PRACTICAL WAYS OF REACHING THE Hip-Hop COMMUNITY FOR CHRIST

- Can students reach their peers for Christ?
- Can students realize that hip-hop has redeeming value and can be used to make a difference for the kingdom of God?
- Can God be glorified through hip-hop?

These questions, along with a few others, are what we asked ourselves as we sought to lay the foundation for The House, Chicago's first all youth and young adult hip-hop church—"the number one church for the streets."

The process of this hip-hop church movement actually started in 1989, when I served as youth pastor of Paseo Baptist Church in Kansas City, Missouri, under the great leadership of Pastor Charles Brisco. At that time our youth ministry hosted two thirty-minute radio shows called *Youth Alternatives* and *How Dat Sound? Christian Rap Countdown* on KPRT Gospel, 1590 AM. Our student leaders were involved in every part of the show's production. Thousands of kids and parents listening to these shows had made call-in responses to our treatment of current issues relevant to the students, brought to them in true hip-hop fashion.

To measure our movement and to bring creative impact, we would host rap outreach concerts for the listeners at skating rinks, parks, schools and other venues. We brought in emcees who follow Christ, such as T-Bone, Gospel Gangstas, SFC (Soldiers for Christ), DOC (Disciples of Christ), Cross Movement and anyone else who was on a mic spitting about the issues on the streets and how the love of Christ can bring us through.

After one event we hosted, students kept asking me, "When you gonna do this again?" Gangbangers who came high and left delivered would ask, "You gonna bring them back nest week?" "How come yawl only do this every once in a while?"

That was when it all started. God put a little irritating, uncomfortable feeling in my spirit, as though there was something else that needed to be done, something nontraditional, that would have impact in the lives of this generation. That "something" was not manifested until August 2004, on the west side of Chicago at Lawndale Community Church, where we sat with ten to fifteen students and young adults who said, "We have been waiting on this. We need this for the youth and young adults in Lawndale."

But to start a hip-hop church is no easy thing. Too many times in Christendom we are too quick to grab hold of the next gimmick and run with it until the leader realizes the people are not excited about this anymore. Look in your church basement, or any church basement, in the storage area, and you will find books, manuals, products, puppet curtains, videos, more manuals on whatever was the trend or fad awhile back—and now that the organizer has moved on or the gimmick proved too hard to pull off, all the stuff has just been put away. Another indication is the famous statement "God led us *for a season* to host a hip-hop church." Tell the truth! The truth is you didn't know what the heck you were getting into!

We cannot be true servants of those in the hip-hop culture and think that they will take us seriously as followers of Christ if we start and stop because we get tired, the cost is too high, or the people are too different. As you consider this ministry, evaluate your heart and determine what you are really trying to do before you embarrass Christ and all who call on his name. All there needs to be is one person, one church, that brings *bad* news instead of good news to the hip-hop culture, and we who believe in this move of God will have to start reexplaining ourselves. If you get excited after reading this book and simply run out to buy some turntables to start a hip-hop church without doing some careful preparation and prayer, you will do the kingdom of God a disservice and you will treat the hip-hop community as just a fad.

For this ministry model to succeed, we all need an EPIC mindset. Leonard Sweet, in his book *Post-modern Pilgrims,* speaks of the EPIC church, which is marked by four characteristics: (1) experiential, (2) participatory, (3) image driven, (4) connected. The church that engages the hip-hop culture is *experiential* in that truth is not just taught but experienced through video, drama and other sensory means. *Participatory* means that the congregation is involved in the service—not just the singing but in what is being done throughout the service. Leaders do ministry *with* rather than ministry *at* or *to.* This church is also *image driven:* its look, the marketing of its message, communicates to the hip-hop generation. The church stays *connected* with hip-hoppers: a connection begins before they enter the service, they feel a connection while they are with you in the service, and there is a follow-up connection afterward.

FIRST KEY: PRAYER

Before The House got started, some friends who had already been making this dream a reality in their ministry had given me counsel: Tommy "Urban D" Kyllonen of Crossover Community Church in Tampa, Florida, the nation's first self-sustaining hip-hop church, and Adam Durso at Christ Tabernacle in New York, with its phenomenal hip-hop youth service Aftershock, held on Friday nights in Queens with lines stretching down the block, where they "represent Christ to the fullest." Both of these brothas reminded me and held me accountable that The House would be only as sustainable as our prayer life was.

If you are seeking to start any type of ministry to influence the emerging generation and the hip-hop culture, the first key to unlock the door is spending time in prayer. This is how we started. In August 2004, on two days a week for one to two hours each day, we prayed. We did not sing, eat, preach, have a lock-in, dance, rap or do anything else but pray. We did this for one month. We did not seek to plan out anything yet but only to labor before God in prayer.

Prayer is the Cinderella of the church: we call on her when the floor needs cleaning. After things have already gone wrong, or if we are too lazy to do anything about a problem, we say, "Let's just pray about it."

Some couples who are engaged already and have the date locked in, plans made, money spent and everything else confirmed, call on the minister at the last minute to do premarital counseling. That is backwards. In that scenario it's tempting to just go through the motions with premarital counseling because so much has already been invested in the wedding. The couple may well just fake it.

Prayer, like premarital counseling, should come first, not last. Prayer is the power for long-lasting change; it is the key that forces us to put up or shut up before God.

So before you even think about planning anything, pull together a team of interested youth, young adults, college students and adults and spend quality time in prayer. In our process, our season of prayer built community amongst the older and younger cats who came out to pray together. In prayer we were able to calm our anxieties and wait for the Lord. Therefore, when the time came to plan the actual service and build the ministry, we had each other's back, front and side to side.

The first step in building a God-led hip-hop ministry, then, is prayer. Here are a few questions you must ask and answer together:

- Is saturation in prayer a central focus of our preparation time?

- Will we focus prayer time on the service only or the people we will be seeking to reach?

- Who *are* we trying to reach?

- How do we pray?

In our team, we prayed for our blocks, for the schools, the gangs, the liquor stores, the police, other churches, and for hearts to be changed, challenged and led to Christ.

Prayer must remain a top priority all the way through the ministry. If you start with prayer as the top priority from the first, this sends a message to the ministry team as it forms and will help all of you to keep prayer as the ongoing focus.

SECOND KEY: THE CORE TEAM

The second key is the development of the leaders who will put this ministry together. This is what we call our Core Team. The House is a church plant of the Evangelical Covenant Church and Lawndale Community Church, and we learned much from both of these ministries about how to put a structure together and reshape it to meet our needs. We held vision-casting meetings so that people who were both curious and seeking to serve could understand what we were seeking to do. From these meetings we gathered the people who were ready to step up and make the ministry happen.

Our Core Team was multiplied into three different segments: structural core team, service core team and prayer team. The structural core team is made up of young adults and high school students who organize behind-the-scenes administration and other activities to build sustainability. Things the structural team handled included the 501(c)(3) not-for-profit-status paperwork, deciding what bank we should use, whether to put together a board of directors. They continue to address important issues: How will we follow up with the students? How will we disciple the students who are already Christians as well as those who make decisions for Christ? How will we market the services?

Our service team has two main responsibilities: to get the word out to their peers and to organize the service. We have broken this down into smaller task teams. The program team is responsible for the flow of the service, who does what and why. The step team practices steps to serve at The House, are dancers, working on synchronized dance moves, breaking and solos. Those involved in drama performances are another team. Emcees (including rappers who are part of our local body and others from the Holy Hip-Hop community in Chicago) come together to work on rhymes and spoken word. We call our emcees Theolyricists. Our One Voice praise team comes together to sing praises in hip-hop style. These ministry teams within the service team are made up of about twenty-five to thirty folks from high school age to young adults. We meet once a week, and of course we start off with prayer and Bible study. Each team is led by an MTL (ministry team leader); these leaders are like a traditional church's deacons. We are trying to change the vernacular as we seek to shift paradigms. We have an MTL over each of the components of the service team (emcees have an MTL, dancers have an MTL, etc.), and they are responsible to teach the Word to their team, pray and develop the gifts of each student.

We will not let anyone serve with us at The House unless they are willing to join one of these teams, seeking to grow in Christ and in their gifts. People from outside the ministry who would like to serve with us are welcome; however, they have to come to our practices and hang out with us twice in the month leading up to the service they will be involved in. We want to meet with them in order to build a relationship, because we need to make sure those outside of our team understand that this is more than you being on stage rapping or dancing, it is about ministry so we can build into each other and others.

Get ready to be inundated with people you have never heard of: as soon as you start something they show up wanting to rap, dance, sing, drop a poem or whatever. But you have to put a standard in place beforehand, so that you can help these cats unlearn old ways of ministry in order to relearn that it is not about you but the kingdom of God.

Our last team is our foundational team, our prayer team. They function behind the scenes, and they also lead in the counseling of people who need prayer and Jesus' work in their life. This team has put together a monthly prayer calendar of thirty-one prayer requests from The House, and others who partner with us receive each day's request and pray in response. The team prays all through the week, and on the night of a service they are there three hours early to pray.

Keep in mind that the structure of your service must fit your church's context. If you have a youth team and/or a young adult ministry, these folks could be interested in helping you to dream this startup with them. You must ask yourselves, *What type of church are we going to be? And who's available to help walk with this vision and build from there?*

THIRD KEY: PROGRAMMING

In any successful church service three major things must happen. First, the Word of God must be priority in the teaching and in the messages through rap and song. Second, the congregation must be involved with the worship; otherwise it will become a spectator sport. Third, throughout the service there must be shifts in communication modes to speak to all the different learning styles.

Gone—or maybe people don't know that they are gone—are the days of just sitting in a sanctuary listening to a sermon without engaging in the service. We have a definition for creativity for The House services: *Creativity is making the familiar strange.* We ask ourselves, *How can we, in every facet of each service, take what people already know about church and worship and the Word and flip it on them so they never knew when they got hit with any of it and yet they are struck with conviction?*

Our program team has put together a few principles that we try to follow as we are planning each service. First, we have a theme for each House Party, and we spend time assessing how to make that theme come off the page. Table 1 is a typical House Party flow schedule.

The service starts with Christian or very clean hip-hop music videos as people are walking in the door and all the lights are off. While the videos play, our logo bounces on the wall in front of the church, just adding eye candy in order to set attendees up for the rest of the service. They will get hit with ten different questions all throughout the night, all having to do with the night's topic. Once the videos are done (about fifteen minutes' worth), either the house emcee or I will step up and hype the crowd with different chants, asking people who is from the West Side and the South Side and throwing CDs out to them. Next we engage the crowd by getting people on the stage to participate in a game.

Sometimes before we welcome everyone we will have a deejay solo or have our emcees hype the crowd up further by getting people who think they can freestyle (rap on the spot with being rehearsed) to come on stage and rhyme. Sometimes we incorporate a comedy clip.

Table 1.

The House Party, October 2, 2004, One-Year Anniversary
Is God Dead?

The main point: The world could know that God is alive if believers died to self. Total dependence on Christ and obedience to his will in our life will cause the world to see that God is alive.

What	Who	Why	How Long
Videos	Tech Team	Crowd warm-up	15 min.
The Game	Phil and House Emcees	Crowd engagement	10/15 min.
Rap	House Emcee	Start the hypeness	1 cut
Dancers	S.O.D. (Spirit of David)	Bring more hypeness	1 dance 5-7 min.
Rap	Holy Culture	Bring more hypeness	15 min.
Poetry	Sofia Gonzalez	Focus toward the Word	2 poems
Singing	Imani & Patients	Mellow it down	2 cuts
Sermon Part 1/ Intro	Pastor Phil	Introduce message	15 min.
Rap	IMOMOS MARROD	Transition from sermon	2 cuts
Dance	Gods Chosen	Bring energy up	1 dance 5-7 min.
Rap	Alpha and Omega	Transitions	2 cuts
Game	Phil/House Emcees	Crowd engagement	10 min.
Offering	Aaron to talk about it	Challenge giving	10 min.
Rap, Freestyle	Holy Culture/Alpha Omega	Open to flow from the offering	10 min.
Dance	House Movement Dancers		
Rap	So Virturs	Bring the hype up	2 cuts
Sermon Part 2/ Body of the text	Pastor Phil	Close message	15 min.
Dance	Genia	Bring focus to the end of the message	7 min.
Closing message	Pastor Phil	Ask folks what are they going to do	10 min.

We use a program called Media Shout, which is like Power-Point on crack. A laptop is attached to an LCD projector (not the old school movie projector), and all throughout the service our logo, various challenging questions and Scriptures are projected. Our tech team (part of our service core team) is responsible for the videos and the Media Shout projection.

When we put the program together, we intentionally seek ways to invite all different types of learners into the service with us—those who are ready to hear the Word while not forgetting those who need to see some type of eye candy.

We plan these services a month in advance, which gives us enough time to plan for crazier stuff. Notice on the service flow that we don't put oral (a poet) right behind a testimony, because that would create a dead zone. There is a need to have a break in the flow after each oral presentation, to create a rhythm that will allow your audience to breathe in between groups, poets and testimonies so that what was just shared is able to stick.

FOURTH KEY: MARKETING

In the hood, everything that is worth something is known by word of mouth—where to buy drugs, who has got the bootleg videos, everything. So you must oversaturate this crowd with information about the service.

At The House we have the baddddddest graphic designer on the planet. He can intuit the look and feel that will get the attention of students in the underground hip-hop community. Every month we print up twenty-five hundred to five thousand "pluggers," and we have our students pass them out all over, in areas that your normal church announcement would not be: bathrooms in the local high schools, the McDonald's around the way, other fast-food joints. "Anywhere, everywhere, all the time" is our motto about marketing our pluggers.

Each week we have the pluggers for the next service ready to pass out to all those who attended the hip-hop service, in order that they can place them in their own areas of influence. We design the plugger to be bilingual: Spanish on one side and English on the other side. A few blocks south of us is Little Village, a very strong Mexican community. We create bilingual pluggers not because the service is going to be bilingual (people assume that most hip-hop events will be in English, though there is a growing group of Spanish-speaking emcees) but in order that first-generation immigrant parents and grandparents can see that our event is related to church and will be less hesitant to let their kids attend. We have found that when the language leaves out the parents, the son or daughter has a harder time trying to explain to them what The House really is.

Finally, one hour before our service, we hit the block with a handful of students to pass out the pluggers to cats who don't have a planner and are not going to remember anything I said to them a month ago. They will consider coming when they are reminded one hour in advance, because they live for the right now, for what is happening now. You must oversaturate your hood first, before you go outside.

Because word of mouth is the main focus of our marketing strategy, we want to push that at every high school and college in our area, but some traditional marketing can be used as well. We are seeking to advertise on the secular station that a lot of young folks in our target demographic listen to. The idea is to have sixty-second commercials that will be almost like a sermonette: I will give a fifty-second story followed by an announcement about The House. A local station may be willing to give you PSAs (public service announcements).

Get used to traveling with a hundred pluggers in your car, in your pocket or purse—you and your team should carry pluggers everywhere you go. Find the local hip-hop clothes shop or the place that sells the most music in the hood, and put your pluggers there, because you want the crowd that would never hear about this through regular Christian circles.

However, *don't* do this if your plugger is lame. In other words don't have a big cross on it or use a bunch of Christian lingo that only Christians understand. If you do that, you'll scare away non-believers. Of course you don't have to make the plugger some booty-shaking thing either. Enough graphics and fonts are available to provide the look you need.

FIFTH KEY: DA WORD

The most important time in the House service is the Word. We have about forty-five minutes of preaching, but you would never realize it is that long because we sprinkle it throughout the service in fifteen-minute increments.

You have got to study the Word in a totally new way, unlearning any comfortable routine you've already developed for sermon study and preparation. You must creatively develop your message so that hip-hoppers will want to listen to what you have to say, almost as if they were calling for an encore at a concert. In order to do this you must move from God's Word and hip-hop culture at the same time. Start with the present, with what is going on now and *why* it is going on, both in your hood and around the globe. Assume your listeners have never even heard of the Bible. That way, by the time you get to the text they are ready to hear you bring the answer. Then you go to the past: this is the Word of God, which, as I just noted, may be unfamiliar with to them. To keep people with you, you need to find a bridge in the text, the material that is relevant to the current situation you've highlighted.

✝

The above are the key components for the development of a hip-hop church. Though each hip-hop church will be unique, my hope is that what I've provided can be a springboard to your own mission, purpose and design.

HIP-HOP MINISTRY OPTIONS

Yo, there are a lot of other ways to engage the hip-hop culture without having a hip-hop church or service. You can use certain elements of this culture to connect with and bring the love of Christ to those within it.

Spoken word. Spoken word is a powerful element in hip-hop. Whether spoken by an emcee or just a poet who is able to drop a hot line, it is one of the most palatable connects for ministry.

Connect with your local high school and talk with the administration about starting a poetry club. You do not want to preach; you just want to be involved with the students who are down with poetry and are willing to learn how to write it, speak it and teach from it. A student from your church may attend that school; she or he could be the contact person to start the poetry club and have insider knowledge of what teacher would be the best sponsor for the club. Every club in every school has to have a sponsoring teacher who agrees to open their room up one day a week for the club's meeting. Together, pick a day of the week when you can be there after school and work with the students as they get their pieces together.

Plan on having the poems showcased in the lunchroom at the end of the semester for two or three days during which each poet can speak their poem to their peers. You can also have the school host an assembly in which the students drop their poems in front of the whole student body.

Your ministry is just to serve, not to suspect, but to guide and love on these students with the gifts they have. Hold back from trying to evangelize everyone; your lifestyle, consistent love for the students and just doing life with them will be your message of Christ.

Deejay classes. Find out from local record stores, national chains or deejay shops how you can get low-cost or free turntables in order to teach students who want to learn deejaying how to spin. Find someone in your church community who spins, and ask them how many days a week they could give to help train some students on the art of deejaying.

Body break classes. Break dancing is back, and it is an untapped ministry opportunity to reach more students. Breakers are very different; they just love to dance, and what you must offer them is a place to dance. You can create a break dance competition. Bring students from all over and offer a cash prize (breakers always want to compete). Once you get their info, pass out info about your break dance classes or just let them know they can use your facility to practice. Watch the movie *You Got Served:* you could put together an outreach similar to that every month (with money or no money). It is just one way you can engage this subculture to connect with the church in a positive way.

Beats and production. Students are increasingly computer and equipment savvy, and they are able to catch on to the working of high-tech equipment and make things happen with it right away. Everyone may not be able to rap, but everyone thinks they can make beats. If you invest, or gather some people who can help you invest, in equipment (iMac computer, different music-making programs and a way to burn the products), you have an instant recording studio. Again, let the entire community know that if anyone wants to make beats and learn to produce, your ministry is offering classes for—for example—five bucks. Charge a fee; I would not offer these classes for free, nor would I make the cost outrageous.

Hip-hop literacy. Out of the need to teach students how to read and to make sense out of life, some ministries have worked with the lyrics of hip-hop. The lyrics you want to use are those that are not offensive and negative but have some substance and meaning. Even with some lyrics that you are unable to pull all the curse words out of, you can challenge students to find better and more creative words to fit in their place. Where the grammar is not well put together, you can teach what the proper grammar should be. You can find lyrics that will have less curse words in the work of artists such as Will Smith and Queen Latifah (some of her newer CDs).

Justice issues. The gospel according to hip-hop is justice. No matter what range of subjects an emcee will rap about, on any of their albums there will be some verse, if not a whole song, dealing with the injustices of the city. So consider gathering students and other young adults to talk about what personal and community issues they find important and what they could do as a team of concerned citizens. Find out how to talk with those in power, and set up an appointment to meet with them.

A group of high school and young adult leaders at The House come together once a month or twice, depending on what is going on, to rally around our issues. We came to a consensus that we wanted the block to be safer, with more police walking and talking with youth service organizations. We set up a meeting with the local district commander and talked with her about our issues. We worked out an agreement: they agreed to our demands, and we agreed to work with some of their concerns. This was a major grassroots movement in which the students saw power shift as they went from just talking about a problem to doing something about it.

Hit the Block outreach concert. Find a vacant lot (there are probably several to choose from in the city) and work with the city to get access to it in order to host a concert. One way you can attract young people is to organize it as a talent show. You might offer a prize that is something important to the youth in the community such as free food, clothes or other items such as a bike. Reach out to local Christian emcees and have them rap in between the students' performances. Now all throughout the concert you are having people share their testimony and preach between the different acts.

Tagging/graffiti classes. Find out through your network who in your neighborhood can tag, graffiti or bomb. Get them on board to teach their skill to other young people on the block. If you can, find a building in your community—even an abandoned building—and get permission to tag a meaningful message on it that the whole block would like and be thankful for. On the boarded-up windows of a house, for example, you could tag families eating dinner on the first floor and kids playing on the second floor.

Entrepreneurship. Teaching business skills can provide the local hip-hop community with realistic expectations for economic independence. A lot of students are going to college to pursue a music business degree with the hope of joining the ranks of P. Diddy, Russell Simmons and others who have major record deals, but these students don't really know where such entrepreneurs had to come from in order to get and be where they are today.

We put flyers into all the high schools and in the course of a semester taught about fifty students the skills of starting a business. Some of the students did try to start and maintain a business, and all fifty were accepted in college; most have graduated, and some are now seeking to start their own business. But the bigger picture was that these young men and women learned some principles that will empower them to earn money and skills to control their money.

Freestyle battles. Now this can be a little edgy if you really want to go there. A freestyle battle involves two emcees going head to head and rapping against each other's skills. Most of the time the words they use are not normally heard in a church; they are very direct and confrontational. You can change the world's methods of battles and create a battle outreach that is different. First, you can require the rappers to sign up the week before and meet with them to discuss the rules that you will enforce, such as no cussing, no sexual reference toward the other person. The second type of battle you can create requires the rappers to rhyme on a topic given to them right there on the stage.

CONCLUSION

Church and Hip-Hop—You Don't Stop

PHIL

Culture and religion cannot be separated! This may come as a shock, but it is true. Each person who is religious, whether they are followers of Christ, Muslim or Jewish, cannot separate themselves from their culture (your beliefs that shape your way of living and thinking). It has been said that great religions and great cultures go together. The biblical understanding is that God is above yet through culture: he transcends and is immanent in culture, exists inside and above culture at the same time. This must be our approach as we unpack how God the Father, Jesus Christ and the Holy Spirit relate to a hip-hop church and why it's important for us to understand and speak to this culture.

You know, it is really ironic that churches and other organizations send people who are from one type of culture to another culture as missionaries, but only after they have learned the language and all the particulars of the culture are they released to reach them—yet many of the same church folks trip out when we talk about hip-hop and God. How can we fail to notice this inconsistency? Don't those within the culture of hip-hop need a clear expression of who Jesus Christ is in their context in order that his love can transform their lives? Instead, because hip-hop is noise to some and anti-everything to others, it becomes demonized. To see the hip-hop church as a missional church that contextualizes the gospel of Christ within that culture becomes impossible for some and heretical for others.

The body of Christ needs to unlearn its prejudices and relearn that hip-hop is spiritual. Because music has spirituality intertwined throughout, hip-hop is spiritual. Spiritual connections are made in hip-hop, in lyrics dealing with the ills of society and in songs about how Jesus walks with me.

The message that is needed if we are to reach the hip-hop culture has to be different from what young people get from a lot of TV preachers, or from preachers around the way who are driving their Lincolns, Jaguars and SUVs while people on the block are starving to death. Hip-hop's perception of the church is all about materialism. An example of this is Cassidy's video "I'm a Hustla," about the "preacher hustle": this is what he sees and what hip-hop culture sees as problems with the African American church. It is seen as hypocritical; the perception is that the church is all about hustling just like everyone else and that there is no difference. Many hip-hoppers are accepting of God and his reality, yet the church's message of the love of Christ is suspect because of its inconsistent modeling in the lives of the body of Christ.

When we seek to form a "hip-hop church," we must stay away from the materialism that can mark both the church and hip-hop as we make use of key elements of hip-hop that speak to this culture. If the worship experience is real, relevant and respectful, young people in the hip-hop culture will likely be able to connect with it. Christ's ministry was incarnational, and we must not lose sight of the fact that we must show that Christ is an everyday Lord to us all. When we exalt Jesus' divine nature to this culture first, without teaching how real he is and how he took on our humanity yet overcame, there is a disconnect.

We are hindered not by what we know but by what we don't

know: this is where hip-hop and the church are similar. There have been so many misrepresentations of Christ, the church and God that those in the hip-hop culture assume they know about Christianity but they really don't know. And the church takes the same position: Christians, thinking they understand the hip-hop culture, lump it all into one pile and are scared to go any further than what they think they know. Thus the hip-hop church or ministry must stand firm if the hip-hop community is to get a new view of the church and its relevance to all of society. Only then will the power of Christ have an impact on the hip-hop culture.

Rap, the element that fuels the message of hip-hop culture, gave me validation that my voice, my life and my block were real and that there was someone who understood me. Hip-hop was able to reach me, teach me and welcomed me into life without any prerequisite of economic status, race or anything else. Hip-hop welcomed me before the church did; it met me where I was at with all my confused understanding of my identity, my lack of self-esteem and my need to fit in. The church, on the other hand, was looking for me to be something I was not, to follow a path that was not yet justified by what I saw in the hood, and to live for a God who was far away and seemingly unconcerned with me unless I got myself together first.

Hip-hop is a way of life. It is the way in which I understand and interpret life, church, God and family. When I see injustices happening in the city, I don't interpret them from the "pull yourself up by your own bootstraps" perspective. When I see a kid getting arrested for selling drugs, my first instinct is to suspect the cops.

Remember the rap from Common? "Told to believe in Jesus / for me he did die / but never ever given / a reason for WHY" ("GOD" on *One Day It Will All Make Sense*).

When I was growing up, this was our anthem. When we heard this song, whether on the radio, on the street or on the block, we would stop and almost give a salute to this song because of the value it put on the life we experienced in the hood. When you feel unable to control the situations around you, people dying, drugs all over and friends getting shot, hopelessness just becomes a way of life, but it helps when you find voices that tell the truth about your life. That is why the movement of hip-hop churches and ministries can make a difference in reaching this culture.

The message of Christ is hip-hop. He came to us, met us where we were and brought us into a right relationship with God. Hip-hop meets the street kid, the suburban kid, right where they are in order to bring them to a place where they can feel esteemed and valued. Even if it doesn't get them paid but gets them out of the ghetto mind trap, it has accomplished its task.

Like any movement, hip-hop's redemption through Christ will take a while. But take note, this is a movement bringing major shifts and transformed mindsets, even in the church. It is a powerful movement when the right people are on board. Will you be so bold as to examine the youth culture around you? And will you seek to empower those who are called to serve the hip-hop community?

EFREM

The church embracing and engaging hip-hop culture in the end is really not about music but about a generation of young people. The key is that hip-hop culture is the soil many young people (especially those who are urban) are growing in. Having a love for hip-hop is not the major issue, the issue is what the church is willing to do because of its love for the hip-hop generation.

God loved the world so much that he invaded it in the form of the Son, Jesus Christ. Jesus came into our world, that people would be healed, delivered, taught, set free and would live eternally with the heavenly Father. What great lengths the Father took because of his love for us! What lengths is the church today willing to go to for young people? Many youth and young adults living in hip-hop culture are in need of healing, freedom, empowerment and the salvation that comes only through Jesus Christ. This time it's the church God is choosing to use for the invasion. I hope you allow God to use your ministry in a revolutionary and biblical manner.

# APPENDIX

Hip-Hop Resources

BOOKS

Lerone Bennett Jr., *Before the "Mayflower": A History of Black America* (Chicago: Johnson Publishers, 2003).

Todd Boyd, *The New H.N.I.C.: The Death of Civil Rights and the Reign of Hip-Hop* (New York: New York University Press, 2002).

————. *Young, Black, Rich, and Famous: The Rise of the NBA, the Hip Hop Invasion, and the Transformation of American Culture* (New York: Doubleday, 2003).

Raquel Cepeda, ed., *And It Don't Stop: The Best American Hip-Hop Journalism of the Last 25 Years* (New York: Faber and Faber, 2004).

Jeff Chang, *Can't Stop, Won't Stop: A History of the Hip-Hop Generation* (New York: St. Martin's Press, 2005).

Francis Davis, *The History of the Blues,* 2nd ed. (Cambridge, Mass.: Da Capo Press, 2003).

Michael Eric Dyson, *Between God and Gangsta Rap: Bearing Witness to Black Culture* (New York: Oxford University Press, 1996).

————, *Holler If You Hear Me: Searching for Tupac Shakur* (New York: Basic Civitas Books, 2001).

Alex Gee and John Teter, J*esus and the Hip-Hop Prophets: Spiritual Insights from Lauryn Hill and Tupac Shakur* (Downers Grove, Ill.: InterVarsity Press, 2003).

Nelson George, *Hip Hop America* (New York: Penguin, 2005).

————, *Post-Soul Nation: The Explosive, Contradictory, Triumphant, and Tragic 1980s as Experienced by African Americans* (New York: Viking, 2004).

Bakari Kitwana, *The Hip-Hop Generation: Young Blacks and the Crisis in African American Culture* (New York: Basic Civitas Books, 2002).

————, *Rap on Gangsta Rap: Who Run It?: Gangsta Rap and Visions of Black Violence* (Chicago: Third World Press, 1994).

————, *Why White Kids Love Hip Hop: Wankstas, Wiggas, Wannabes, and the New Reality of Race in America* (New York: Basic Civitas Books, 2005).

Anthony Pinn, ed., *Noise and Spirit: The Religious and Spiritual Sensibilities of Rap Music* (New York: New York University Press, 2003).

Tricia Rose, *Black Noise: Rap Music and Black Culture in Contemporary America* (Hanover, N.H.: University Press of New England, 1994).

Russell Simmons with Nelson George, *Life and Def: Sex, Drugs, Money, and God* (New York: Crown Publishers, 2001).

CHRISTIAN HIP-HOP EVENTS (ANNUAL)

Rap Fest in the summer in the BX: Straight-up righteous hip-hop for twelve hours. Christian rappers, breakers. There's nothing like it in the U.S. See <www.rapfest.com>.

Flavor Fest Tampa Florida: first weekend in November. Workshops and concerts with major artists; great time of peeping Christ in every element of hip-hop <www.Flavoralliance.com>.

MOVIES/VIDEOS

Beat Street (1984)
Belly (1998)
Boyz in the Hood (1991)
Breakin' (1984)
Brown Sugar (2002)
8Mile (2002)
Freestyle (2005)
Fresh (2002)
Juice (2001)
Krush Groove (1985)
The MC—Why We Do It (2004)
New Jersey Drive (1995)
Tupac: Resurrection (2003)
The Spook Who Sat by the Door (2004)
We Got Your Kids (2003) <www.wegotyourkids.com>
Wild Style (1983)
You Got Served (2004)

MAGAZINES (CHRISTIAN)

Mic Rippaz HHH Magazine <www.micrippaz.com>
Feed <www.feedstop.com>
Rapzilla <www.rapzilla.com>
What's the Word <www.wtwmagazine.com>

MINISTRIES

Beats and Blessings: Hip-hop ministry based in New Life Fellowship Church in Elmhurst, Queens, New York. Youth directors Craig and Zola Allen.
www.beatsandblessings.com

Cross Movement Ministries
www.crossmovement.com

Crossover Community Church: At <www.crossoverchurch.org> and <www.flavoralliance.com> you can see the many resources this church offers including hip-hop praise and worship CDs complete with instrumental tracks for singers to sing with if you don't have a deejay or hip-hop musicians.

The House Covenant Church
www.thehouse.org

The Sanctuary Covenant Church
www.sanctuarycovenant.org
www.sancturarycdc.org (Community Development Corps.)

Sound Changers: This ministry located in Carey, North Carolina, is committed to equipping the African American church to reach youth and young adults living in hip-hop culture.

Urban Street Level Ministries: A hip-hop praise and worship ministry located in the Washington, D.C., area. The founders, Elwood and Betty Jones, are available for workshops and speaking as well. Check out their website at <www.uslmusic.com> or <www.usl.com>.

RADIO (GOSPEL HIP-HOP)
Eprayze radio <www.eprayseradio.com>
Holy Culture radio <www.holycultureradio.com>
Radio U <www.radiou.com>

RECORD LABELS
Cross Movement Records <www.crossmovementrecords.com>
www.flavoralliance.com
Gotee Records

WEBSITE
www.hiphopzone.com

OTHER RESOURCES

Hip-Hop Bible
Fred Lynch, *The Epic: A Hip-Hop Version of the Gospel of John*
For more information, check out <www.gettheepic.com>.

Real: a hip-hop-influenced Biblezine, published by Thomas Nelson.

Hip-Hop Devotional
Elements of Life: from the American Bible Society, a very well-written hip-hop style devotional, <http://www.americanbible.org/site/News2?page=NewsArticle&id=529>.

The Verbs is one of the hottest hip-hop devotionals out there. It's a CD that combines Scripture and hip-hop to present everyday nuggets of truth to equip youth and young adults. The cost is $10, and the CD can be ordered from The Shelter UYC, 8210 Ridgeland, Chicago, IL 60617, phone: 773-791-1935.

Check out the entire book of Ecclesiastes in an artistic, hip-hop paraphrase of Scripture. Fred Lynch has hooked this piece up so you can use this for your ministry everyday. Check it out at <www.Godstyle.com>.

Hip-Hop Humor
Note: many of these are loaded with profanity so you will have to choose clips carefully and consider what works in your context.

Bertrice Berry and Joan Coker, *Sckraight from the Ghetto: You Know You're Ghetto If* (New York: St. Martin's Press, 1996).
Bertrice Berry, *You Still Ghetto: You Know You're Still Ghetto If* (New York: St. Martin's Press, 1998).
Chris Rock, any of his DVDs
Chappelle's Show on Comedy Central
The Fresh Prince (Complete first and second seasons available

on DVD or the whole series is available on video)
In Living Color (Seasons 1-4 available on DVD)
Martin Lawrence: You So Crazy DVD
Yo' Mama books by Snap C. Pop and Kid Rank
  Yo' Mama! Bust-O-Pedia (New York: Berkley Books, 1995).
  Mo' Yo' Mama! Bust-O-Pedia (New York: Berkley Books, 1996).
  Even Mo' Yo' Mama! (New York: Kensington Books, 1997).
  Yo' Mama! Uncensored (New York: Kensington Books, 1999).